The Seeker's Gold

Unlocking Life's Greatest Treasure

Unravelling the Illusions of Power, Love, and Destiny on the Path to True Fulfilment.

SHREE SHAMBAV

The Seeker's Gold
Unlocking Life's Greatest Treasure
Shree Shambav

Published by Shree Shambav, Tamil Nadu, India
Shree Shambav Ink & Imagination "Where Words Breathe and Imagination Soars"
All Rights Reserved

First Edition, 2025

Copyright © 2025, Muniswamy Rajakumar

All rights reserved. No part of this publication may be reproduced, distributed, or transmitted in any form or by any means, including photocopying, recording, or other electronic or mechanical methods, without the author's prior written permission. It is illegal to copy this book, post it to a website, or distribute it by any other means without permission.

The request for permission should be addressed to the author.

ISBN: 978-93-342-9485-9

Email:shreeshambav@gmail.com
Web:www.shambav.org

DEDICATION

"Isavasyam idam sarvam yat kim ca jagatyam jagat, tena tyaktena bhunjitha, ma gridhah kasyasvid dhanam"

To the Almighty,

the Divine Masters,

the family who listens,

and my parents who see –

your presence shapes the pages of my life's journey.

"Isavasyam idam sarvam yat kim ca jagatyam jagat"

Meaning: "God encompasses everything you perceive, see, or touch with your sense organs."

DISCLAIMER

Transforming Life is a guide intended to inspire self-reflection, personal growth, and spiritual exploration. The insights, teachings, and practices shared in this book are based on spiritual principles, philosophical interpretations, and collective wisdom.

The Seeker's Gold – Unlocking Life's Greatest Treasure is a profound and transformative tale of one dreamer's relentless pursuit of power, wealth, and wisdom. Driven by an enigmatic vision, the seeker embarks on a journey to unearth a hidden treasure. But as the path unfolds, what begins as a quest for material riches soon becomes a pilgrimage of the soul. Encounters with wise mentors, trials of love and loss, and the fleeting illusions of success reveal a deeper truth—the greatest treasure is not found but realised.

Divided into distinct parts, this book explores the fundamental pillars of human existence—love, ambition, sacrifice, freedom, and the eternal search for meaning. With each challenge faced and lesson learned, the seeker discovers that fulfilment does not lie in possessions or status but in understanding the very essence of life itself.

Rich in allegory and timeless wisdom, *The Seeker's Gold* is more than just a story—it is an invitation. A call to embark on your own journey of self-discovery, to question, to reflect, and to unlock the most valuable treasure of all—the truth within.

Disclaimer

The author and publisher disclaim all liability for any outcomes, direct or indirect, arising from the interpretation or application of the concepts explored in this book. The insights shared are meant for inspiration and contemplation, not as professional advice in financial, psychological, legal, or spiritual matters.

Engaging with this material is an act of personal exploration. True transformation requires mindfulness, discernment, and self-responsibility. This book does not promise specific results, nor does it claim to hold universal truths. It merely offers perspectives—some may resonate, and others may not. Take what aligns with your journey, leave what does not, and trust in your own path.

We are honoured to accompany you on this journey. May the insights within these pages inspire you to live with greater clarity, purpose, and connection. Let this book be a catalyst for your own transformation, revealing the hidden gold that has always been within you.

Note - If any part of the book, in any sequence, hurts the reader's sentiments, it would be just out of a sheer accident not intentional

EPIGRAM

The Seeker's Gold

"Gold may fill your hands, but only wisdom can fill your soul. The true treasure is not found in what we possess, but in what we become."

– Shree Shambav

The Seeker's Gold

Unlocking Life's Greatest Treasure

Shree Shambav

Shree Shambav is a 33x best-selling author renowned for his transformative works in personal development and spiritual growth.

Dear Cherished Readers

Dear Cherished Readers,

As I embark on this new literary voyage, my heart swells with profound gratitude and an overwhelming sense of connection. With deep emotion, I extend my heartfelt appreciation to each of you who has joined me on this journey.

With sincere warmth, I invite you to revisit the steps we have taken together through the pages of my earlier works. Our odyssey began with "Journcy of Soul - Karma," a book that marked my first foray into the world of words and a testament to the raw passion that ignited my writing adventure.

The subsequent chapters of our shared narrative unfolded through the enchanting tapestry of the "Twenty + One" series. Each page turned was a brushstroke on the canvas of our imaginations, painting vivid stories that I hoped would resonate deeply within your hearts.

And how can I forget the transformative journey we embarked on with the "Life Changing Journey - Inspirational Quotes Series." Day by day, quote by quote, we delved into reflections that uplifted, inspired, and sought to bring a glimpse of light to our souls.

The release of "Death - Light of Life and the Shadow of Death" promises to shed new light on the timeless mystery of death. Similarly, "Unleashing the Incredible Potential of Programming with Python - Optimum - PYTHON: Ultimate Guide for Beginners Series I" is poised to empower readers with newfound knowledge.

In addition, my technical book, OPTIMUM Python Series II - Exploring Data Structures and Algorithms, delves into advanced concepts in Python programming, offering a comprehensive guide for those seeking to deepen their understanding.

OPTIMUM – Python Power Series III is your essential guide to mastering the most powerful Python libraries for data science. From data manipulation and visualisation to machine learning, this book empowers you with practical tools to solve real-world challenges. Unleash your potential and transform the way you work with data

Shree Shambav expands his artistic repertoire with "*Whispers of Eternity: A Symphony of Soulful Verses,*" a heartfelt exploration of the human experience. Alongside this, his "*Whispers of the Soul: A Journey Through Haiku*" distils profound insights into poignant verses. Together, these works showcase his versatility and mastery of soulful expression, inviting readers on a journey of self-discovery. Through his poetry, he weaves a rich tapestry of emotion that resonates deeply with the heart.

Shree Shambav's latest works—*Learn to Love Yourself: A Journey of Discovering Inner Beauty and Strength Through 10 Transformative Rules, The Power of Letting Go: Embrace Freedom and Happiness, A Journey of Lasting Peace*—are true treasures of self-discovery, *The*

Entitlement Trap: Get Over It, Get On, Whispers of a Dying Soul: Unspoken Regrets and Unlived Dreams, Whispers of Silence - Unlocking Inner Power through Stillness, The Power of Words: Transforming Speech, Transforming Lives, The Art of Intentional Living: Minimalism for a Life of Purpose, Awakening the Infinite: The Power of Consciousness in Transforming Life, Beyond the Veil: A Journey Through Life After Death series, Bonds Beyond Blood - Where love builds bridges, and bonds defy blood., A Journey into Spiritual Maturity - 12 Golden Rules for Inner Transformation, and The Inner Battlefield - Overcoming the Enemies of the Mind and Soul.

In addition to these works, Shree Shambav has recently ventured into astrology with the release of Astrology Unveiled – Foundations of Ancient Wisdom Series I to VI, expanding into the realm of metaphysics. These books explore the foundational principles of Vedic astrology, offering readers a rich and practical understanding of this ancient wisdom.

Your unwavering support, enthusiasm to immerse yourself in my writings, and readiness to embark on these journeys with me have been my greatest sources of inspiration. Your input has been a beacon guiding me through the creation process, moulding these stories into containers of passion, emotion, knowledge, and resonance.

As I unveil this new narrative before you, know that your presence, insights, and shared moments have been my companions. The path we have walked together is etched in the annals of my creative evolution, and it's an honour beyond words to have you by my side once more.

Here's to the readers who have illuminated my path with their presence, who have embraced my stories with open hearts, and who have woven themselves into the very fabric of my literary world. Our journey has been a symbiotic dance of writer and reader, a harmony of souls brought together by the magic of storytelling.

With a heart brimming with appreciation and eyes glistening with anticipation, I extend my deepest gratitude for your unwavering support. Thank you for the memories, the shared emotions, and the countless hours spent in the worlds we've crafted together. As we step into this new adventure, let's continue to explore, feel, and discover the boundless horizons that words can unveil.

Warmly,

Shree Shambav

THE SEEKER'S GOLD

Suggested Reads

FROM BEST-SELLING AUTHOR

Endorsements

"A breathtaking journey into the heart of human ambition, struggle, and transformation. This book is more than a story—it is a mirror reflecting our deepest desires and greatest fears. With each chapter, it guides us through the illusions of wealth and power, only to unveil the real treasure hidden within: wisdom, love, and purpose. A must-read for anyone seeking meaning beyond material success."

— Pooja

PREFACE

There comes a moment in every life when the soul whispers a question—Is this all there is? The pursuit of wealth, power, and success promises fulfillment, yet the deeper we chase them, the more we sense an emptiness lurking beneath. We measure our worth in gold, in titles, in fleeting triumphs, only to find that none of it truly satisfies the hunger within. What if the greatest treasure is not something we acquire, but something we awaken to?

This is the story of a seeker—someone who dares to leave behind the familiar in search of something greater. The journey is filled with trials of ambition and failure, love and loss, and hope and despair. Along the way, teachers appear in unexpected forms: a stranger's wisdom, a fleeting love, a painful betrayal, a moment of silence beneath the stars. Each experience strips away illusions and reveals a truth long forgotten—what we seek is not out there, but has been within us all along.

Through the twists and turns of this adventure, this book explores the timeless questions that shape our existence:

- Is wealth a tool for freedom or a trap of the ego?
- Can love and ambition walk hand in hand?

- Is suffering a punishment, or the gateway to transformation?

- What does it mean to truly live before we die?

"The Seeker's Gold – Unlocking Life's Greatest Treasure" is not just a tale of one journey—it is the story of every person who has ever questioned the meaning of their path. It is an invitation to step beyond the known, to challenge the beliefs we cling to, and to uncover the wisdom that has always been waiting.

If you have ever felt that life holds something deeper, something richer than what the world has shown you—then the journey begins now.

With gratitude and encouragement,

Shree Shambav

INTRODUCTION

There is a moment in every life when the illusion shatters. The things once chased with relentless passion—wealth, status, power, love—begin to lose their luster. The victories that once seemed so significant feel hollow. The relationships that once felt unbreakable slip through our fingers. The meaning we thought we had built crumbles beneath the weight of an unspoken question:

Have I been searching in the wrong places?

This is the journey of the seeker, the one who dares to leave behind the comforts of certainty to chase something far more elusive—truth. It is not an easy path. The world rewards those who conform, who accept the pursuit of material success as the ultimate purpose of life. But for those who cannot ignore the whisper of something more, the road unfolds in ways both beautiful and brutal. It challenges, transforms, and, in the end, reveals what was hidden all along: the greatest treasure is not something we find, but something we become.

The Journey Unfolds

This book is not just a story; it is an odyssey of the soul. Divided into six parts, it mirrors the stages of every true transformation.

PART ONE – The Call to Destiny

Every great journey begins with a whisper—a dream, a longing, a call that refuses to fade. Aryan's restless soul is haunted by visions of treasure, pulling him away from the comforts of the known. But every step into the unknown demands sacrifice, courage, and an unshakable belief that something greater awaits. Yet, does the call of destiny lead to fulfilment or merely to another mirage in the desert of ambition?

PART TWO – Love, Loss, and Learning

Love is the most powerful force in existence—it builds, destroys, and transforms. Aryan's path is shaped by love in its many forms: romantic, familial, and the silent love of those who guide him in unseen ways. But love also teaches through loss, reminding him that nothing is truly his to keep. Through joy and heartbreak, he learns that the greatest lessons do not come from conquest but from the people who walk beside us, even if only for a while.

PART THREE – The Rise to Power and Fame

Wealth, influence, and power—once distant dreams—become Aryan's reality. He masters the art of strategy, builds empires, and commands respect. But with every rise, there is a shadow. The world applauds success but does not warn of its cost. Pleasure is fleeting, indulgence deceives, and the walls built to protect often become prisons. When ambition has been conquered, what remains?

PART FOUR – The Cost of Power

Power demands more than it gives. Justice becomes a question of perspective, freedom proves to be an illusion, and the mind and heart engage in a battle that leaves no true victor. Pain carves deeper wisdom, and the truths that were once ignored now refuse to be silenced. Aryan must face the hardest truth of all—was the journey worth the price he paid?

PART FIVE – Finding What Was Never Lost

The search that began with a dream of treasure leads to something far greater. Friendships, faith, and purpose emerge as the real wealth of existence. Silent prayers guide Aryan toward a truth he had been too blind to see. In the end, was he ever truly lost, or had he simply forgotten the path home?

PART SIX – The Final Treasure

The greatest revelations do not come at the peak of power but at its decline. As Aryan returns home, he finds a world changed beyond recognition. Loved ones lost, promises unfulfilled, time unrelenting. But in the ashes of the past, a final truth is whispered—what we seek in distant lands has always been within us. The real treasure was never gold or glory, but the wisdom earned, the love shared, and the soul that remains when everything else is stripped away.

The Treasure Awaits

This is not just one person's journey. It is your journey. It is the path walked by anyone who has ever questioned the world, by anyone who has ever felt lost, by anyone who has ever dared to ask, "Is there more?"

There is.

The gold you seek is not buried beneath the earth or locked within vaults. It is waiting in the depths of your being, hidden behind your fears, buried beneath your desires, veiled by the distractions of the world.

Are you ready to uncover it? Let the journey begin.

With warmth and sincerity,

Shree Shambav

PROLOGUE

There comes a moment in life when the noise fades. The ambitions, the desires, the endless striving—suddenly, they seem distant, as if belonging to someone else. And in that moment of silence, a single question arises:

Was it all worth it?

The world teaches us to chase wealth, power, recognition, and love. We are told that fulfillment lies in accumulation, that success is measured in what we possess, and that happiness is found in reaching the next milestone. And so, we run. We run after careers, after relationships, after achievements. We run, believing that if we just acquire enough, achieve enough, become enough—then, at last, we will feel whole.

But what happens when we reach the summit and find the view disappointing? What happens when we touch the treasure we spent years seeking, only to realise it does not fill the emptiness inside?

This is the story of every seeker—the one who dares to question, who risks everything to find something real. It is a journey not just through distant lands but through the landscapes of the soul. It is a story of love and loss, ambition and surrender, pain and awakening. It is about learning that the greatest treasures are never found where we expect and that sometimes, we must lose ourselves to truly be found.

This book is not merely a tale—it is a mirror. It reflects the illusions we cling to, the dreams we chase, and the truths we resist. It challenges the definitions of success, love, and happiness we have been given, asking us to strip away the superficial and discover what truly matters.

If you have ever felt the ache of something missing… if you have ever reached the peak of achievement and still felt unfulfilled… if you have ever looked at your life and wondered, "Is this all there is?"—then this journey is for you.

The treasure you seek is waiting.

But first, you must dare to seek.

CONTENTS

DEDICATION iii
DISCLAIMER v
EPIGRAM vii
Dear Cherished Readers xi
Suggested Reads xv
Endorsements xvii
PREFACE xix
INTRODUCTION xxi
PROLOGUE xxv
CONTENTS xxvii
The Wind of Destiny 1
PART ONE 1
   The Call to Destiny 1
CHAPTER I 1
   The Dream That Wouldn't Fade 1
CHAPTER II 5
   Leaving the Known Behind 5
PART TWO 11
   Love, Loss, and Learning 11
CHAPTER III 13
   The Unseen Power of Love 13

- **CHAPTER IV** 19
  - The Sacred Bond of Marriage 19
- **CHAPTER V** 25
  - Children: Our Greatest Teachers 25
- **PART THREE** 31
  - The Rise to Power and Fame 31
- **CHAPTER VI** 33
  - Mastering Wealth and Influence 33
- **CHAPTER VII** 39
  - The Art of Strategy 39
- **CHAPTER VIII** 43
  - The Gift of Giving 43
- **CHAPTER IX** 47
  - Indulgence and Its Illusions 47
- **CHAPTER X** 53
  - The Dance of Joy and Sorrow 53
- **CHAPTER XI** 57
  - The Weight of Walls 57
- **CHAPTER XII** 61
  - The Illusion of Control 61
- **CHAPTER XIII** 65
  - Beyond the Fabric of Identity 65
- **PART FOUR** 73
- **CHAPTER XIV** 75

The Cost of Power 75
CHAPTER XV 79
Justice Beyond Revenge 79
CHAPTER XVI 85
The Paradox of Laws 85
CHAPTER XVII 89
Freedom and Its Hidden Chains 89
CHAPTER XVIII 93
The Battle Between Heart and Mind 93
CHAPTER XIX 97
The Gift Hidden in Pain 97
PART FIVE 101
Finding What Was Never Lost 101
CHAPTER XX 103
The Fragility of Friendship 103
CHAPTER XXI 109
The Power of Silent Prayers 109
CHAPTER XXII 113
The Journey from Pleasure to Purpose 113
PART SIX 119
The Final Treasure 119
CHAPTER XXIII 121
The Journey's End 121
CHAPTER XXIV 127

The Island of Echoes	127
CHAPTER XXV	**135**
Whispers of Destiny	135
CHAPTER XXVI	**139**
The Haunting of Unfinished Journeys	139
CHAPTER XXVII	**145**
The Echo of the Unseen	145
CHAPTER XXVIII	**151**
The Path to Gorgons	151
CHAPTER XXIX	**157**
Whispers of the Forgotten Land	157
CHAPTER XXX	**163**
The Phantom of the Dunes	163
CHAPTER XXXI	**167**
The Threshold of Destiny	167
CHAPTER XXXII	**171**
The Mirror of Truth	171
CHAPTER XXXIII	**177**
The Final Journey Home	177
CHAPTER XXXIV	**183**
The Journey Ends, The Journey Begins	183
CHAPTER XXXV	**187**
The Return Home	187
CHAPTER XXXVI	**193**

The Last Promise	193
CHAPTER XXXVII	197
The Journey's True End	197
Life Coach and Philanthropist	205
ACKNOWLEDGEMENTS	207

The Wind of Destiny

"Destiny does not shout; it whispers. Only those who dare to listen will hear its call. Only those who dare to follow will find its truth."

- Shree Shambav

The night was still, yet a storm raged within. The stars above shimmered like scattered gold, but no wealth in the world could calm the restless heart that beat beneath the open sky. A longing, a hunger—not just for riches, but for something unseen, something beyond. A whisper of destiny called from the depths of the unknown.

A dream had taken root, vivid and unshakable—a treasure buried beyond distant mountains, beyond the grasp of ordinary men. Was it fortune or fate? Was it a vision of material wealth or something far more profound? The only way to know was to begin the journey.

The path ahead was uncertain. Shadows of doubt loomed large, and the weight of expectations pressed heavily. The world had always measured success in gold, in power, in status. But what if the true measure of wealth lay elsewhere? What if the journey itself was the treasure?

Every great story begins with a choice. Stay bound to the comfort of the known, or step into the unknown and seek the truth.

With nothing but a heart full of questions and a soul eager for answers, the journey begins.

Beyond riches, beyond dreams—what truly awaits at the end of the road?

And so, the seeker takes the first step…

The First Step into the Unknown

The air in the village felt different that morning. The sun had risen like it always did, casting its golden glow over the rooftops, warming the narrow streets where children played and merchants prepared for the day's trade. Yet, to Aryan, everything seemed distant—like an echo of a life he no longer belonged to. His heart was heavy with the weight of choice, and his mind buzzed with questions that had no easy answers.

The old man's words had not left him. They clung to him like a lingering fragrance, both comforting and unsettling. *Not all dreams are mere illusions… some are whispers of destiny.*

But how did one follow a whisper?

Aryan had spent the night thinking. The dream had come to him again, clearer than before. The lone tree, the buried chest, the winds whispering his name—it all felt more real than the ground beneath his feet. And yet, he had nothing. No map, no plan, no certainty that the treasure even existed beyond the chambers of his own imagination.

How does one begin the pursuit of greatness? Is it with a carefully laid plan, or does it begin in surrender—stepping into the unknown, trusting the path to reveal itself?

The villagers had always spoken of dreamers in hushed tones, with equal parts admiration and pity. *"He has his head in the clouds,"* they would say. *"Dreaming is for those who don't know the weight of reality."* Aryan had once believed them. But now, he wasn't so sure.

His father, a man of quiet strength, sat on the wooden steps of their modest home, sharpening his sickle. He had always lived by simple truths—the land provides, the family sustains, and a man's duty is to remain steadfast. When Aryan hesitated at the doorway, his father looked up.

"You've been lost in thought, son." His father's voice was steady, yet there was an edge to it—a knowing. "I see it in your eyes. The same look your grandfather had before he left."

Aryan swallowed. He had never met his grandfather, only heard the stories. A man who had once walked away from the village in search of something greater—something beyond the ordinary. Some said he had found it, others whispered that he had been swallowed by the world, never to return.

"Did you think he was a fool?" Aryan asked carefully.

His father stopped sharpening the blade. For a long moment, he said nothing. Then, with a sigh, he met Aryan's gaze. "A fool? No. A dreamer? Yes. But dreams, Aryan, are like fire. They can warm you, or they can consume you. The difference is in how you tend to them."

The words settled deep into Aryan's chest. "And what if I choose to follow mine?"

His father exhaled through his nose, wiping the blade clean. "Then you must be willing to walk through the fire. And you must ask yourself—what matters more, the dream or the journey?"

Aryan didn't answer. He didn't have an answer.

But later, as he stood at the edge of the village, a single bag slung over his shoulder, he knew that the choice had already been made.

His mother clutched his hands, her eyes shining with unspoken fears. "Will you come back?" she whispered.

"I don't know," Aryan admitted. "But I promise, I will not forget where I come from."

She pressed something into his palm—a small pendant, worn with time. "Your grandfather carried this. He said it was a reminder... that no matter how far you go, home is never lost."

Aryan closed his fingers around it, feeling the warmth of her touch still lingering.

The old man was waiting for him at the edge of the road. He said nothing, only nodded in quiet approval.

Aryan took a breath, the last breath of the life he had known. And then, with a single step forward, he left behind the certainty of yesterday for the mystery of tomorrow.

For some, dreams are fleeting fantasies. For others, they are whispers of destiny.

What separated the dreamers from the seekers was a single step.

And Aryan had taken his.

PART ONE

The Call to Destiny

"The journey is never about reaching the treasure—it is about becoming the one who no longer needs it."

- Shree Shambav

CHAPTER I

The Dream That Wouldn't Fade

"A dream is not a feather that drifts aimlessly in the wind—it is a stone carried in the heart. It will either anchor you in fear or become the foundation upon which you build your destiny."

- Shree Shambav

The Dream That Wouldn't Fade

The night was quiet, yet within Aryan, a storm raged. He lay on his small wooden bed, staring at the thatched roof above him, his mind consumed by the dream that had visited him again. It was always the same—golden sands stretching endlessly, an ancient chest buried beneath a lone tree, the whisper of the wind calling his name. But this was no ordinary dream. It did not fade with the morning light like all others. It clung to his soul, leaving an ache, an unspoken promise that somewhere beyond the horizon, something awaited him.

Aryan had always felt different. While the people of his village were content tending to their fields and livestock, he longed for more. He could not silence the voice inside that told him he was meant for greatness. Yet, how could he explain this to those around him? His father, a man of simple wisdom, would only shake his head and say, "A man's worth is in the work he does, not in the dreams he chases." His mother would look at him with worry, fearing that this restlessness in his heart would lead him away from home, perhaps never to return.

But how could he ignore a dream that refused to leave him? It was not an illusion, not a fleeting fantasy—it was a calling. He could feel it in his bones.

One evening, as he sat by the village well, lost in thought, an old man with piercing eyes and a presence that demanded attention approached him. His robes were worn with time, yet his gaze held the weight of someone who had seen more than most. The old man sat beside Aryan without a word, as if he had been waiting for this moment.

"You've seen it, haven't you?" the old man finally spoke, his voice carrying the depth of distant lands.

Aryan's breath caught. "Seen what?" he asked, though he knew what the man meant.

"The treasure," the old man said simply. "The one buried beneath the lone tree in the golden sands."

Aryan's heart pounded. "How do you know about that?"

The old man chuckled. "Because every seeker sees it before they embark on their journey." He leaned closer, his voice turning softer, as if revealing a secret. "Not all dreams are mere illusions, boy. Some are whispers of destiny."

Aryan shivered. "Then why me?"

The old man smiled, his eyes twinkling with a knowing sadness. "The real question is not why you have the dream, but whether you have the courage to follow it."

Aryan swallowed hard. He had spent years yearning for something beyond his ordinary life, but now that the path was opening before him, doubt crept in. The village was safe, predictable. Beyond it lay uncertainty, danger, the unknown.

"What if I fail?" Aryan whispered, more to himself than to the old man.

The old man placed a weathered hand on Aryan's shoulder. "A man who never leaves the shore will never know the vastness of the ocean."

Aryan stared into the distance. His heart was still restless, but now it burned with a new fire—a fire that would either consume him or forge him into something greater.

The dream had never been just a dream. It had been a call. And for the first time, Aryan realised he had only two choices: ignore it and live in regret, or step forward and embrace whatever fate had in store.

And so, under the watchful eyes of the old man, Aryan made a silent vow.

He would seek the treasure.

He would seek his destiny.

CHAPTER II

Leaving the Known Behind

"We live as if we have forever, yet time slips through our fingers like sand. The question is not how much time we have, but what we choose to do with the moments given to us."

— Shree Shambav

The morning air was crisp, carrying with it the scent of damp earth and distant rain. Aryan stood at the edge of the village, where the cobbled streets met the wild, untamed road stretching beyond the horizon. His heart pounded—not with fear, but with the weight of choice.

Behind him, the life he had always known whispered in comforting familiarity. The old baker, Ramji, was already at work, his laughter rolling like thunder as he shared jokes with the farmers. The temple bells rang in their usual rhythm, marking yet another predictable day in the only world Aryan had ever known.

Ahead of him, the unknown loomed. The road was empty, a path carved by those who had once dared to leave and never returned. It was not just a road—it was a question. A challenge. A whisper in the wind asking, *Are you truly ready?*

He tightened the straps of his worn satchel, glancing once more at his home—the small mud house where he had spent countless nights dreaming of greatness, staring at the stars as if they held the secrets of his destiny.

His mother stood at the doorstep, her eyes filled with the sorrow of unspoken words. "You don't have to go, Aryan," she said softly.

"I do, Amma," he replied, his voice steady, though his heart ached. "The dream won't let me rest."

She sighed, wiping her hands on her sari. "Dreams are strange things, my son. They can either show you the path or lead you astray."

Aryan took a deep breath. "And I will never know which unless I walk it."

Beside him, his childhood friend, Rohan, shook his head. "Why search for something that may not even exist? What if the treasure is just a fantasy? What if you lose everything and return with nothing?"

Aryan smiled, but there was steel in his voice. "Then at least I will return knowing I had the courage to seek."

The village elder, Baba Govind, had been silently observing from under the shade of the banyan tree. His voice, when it came, was like the rustling of old parchment. "To leave the known behind is not the hardest part, my boy. It is to walk forward when doubt grips you, when the weight of the past calls you back. The road ahead will not just test your feet—it will test your soul."

Aryan nodded. He had already made his choice, but choices came with sacrifices. He knelt, touching his forehead to the earth, offering a silent prayer to the land that had raised him.

Then, without another word, he turned and took his first step toward the unknown.

The world did not change in that instant. The village did not vanish behind him. But something within him shifted—like the first crack in a dam before the flood. He was no longer just a dreamer. He was a seeker.

The Crossroads of Destiny

The wind carried voices—some soft as a mother's lullaby, others sharp as the warning of a storm. They whispered in Aryan's ears, curling around his thoughts, weaving doubt into his resolve.

"Is true transformation possible without stepping away from comfort?"

His fingers brushed against the satchel slung over his shoulder—a bag filled with little more than hope and uncertainty. Behind him, the village stood bathed in the golden glow of dawn, the air thick with the scent of freshly baked bread and burning incense. It was a place where he had laughed, loved, and lived within the safe walls of familiarity.

And yet, his heart ached—not with the fear of leaving, but with the unbearable weight of staying.

"Perhaps not," the whispers seemed to answer. *"Perhaps growth demands that we break the shell of familiarity and walk barefoot into uncertainty."*

The path before him was not just a road of dust and stone—it was the edge of everything he had ever known. Beyond it lay a world untamed, filled with both promise and peril. His feet, steady yet hesitant, hovered at the threshold of the unknown.

"How do we recognise when it's time to leave behind the familiar and embrace the uncertain?"

He closed his eyes. In the silence, the answer stirred within him.

Maybe it is when the dream becomes louder than the fear, when the fire inside burns too fiercely to be ignored.

Maybe it is when the longing for *more* outgrows the contentment of *enough*.

Or maybe, just maybe, it is when staying where we are feels more painful than the risk of leaving.

He took a breath, deep and full, letting the air of home fill his lungs one last time. Then, with the courage of a man stepping beyond the edge of certainty, Aryan took his first step into the unknown.

The Threshold of Fate

Behind him lay the life he had always known—the scent of damp earth after rain, the sound of cattle bells in the distance, the voices of neighbours who had seen him grow from a boy into a young man. Their expectations clung to him like unseen chains, whispering all the reasons he should stay.

Yet, the pull of the road ahead was stronger. It was not just a path of dust and stone; it was the whisper of a destiny not yet written. But standing there, caught between what was and what could be, a question gnawed at him:

"Does the fear of losing what we have outweigh the potential of what we can become?"

He clenched his fists. He had spent nights staring at the wooden beams of his small home, wondering if his dreams were mere illusions. A simple life awaited him if he stayed—a predictable one. Was that not enough?

A rustling behind him. A voice.

"You hesitate, boy."

Aryan turned. Elder Suraj stood by the well, his weathered face half-hidden beneath the shade of his tattered hood. His eyes, though old, still burned with the sharpness of a man who had seen far too much.

"You fear what lies ahead," Suraj continued, stepping forward. *"But tell me, are you more afraid of the unknown… or of never knowing what could have been?"*

Aryan lowered his gaze.

The elder sighed, settling onto a nearby rock. *"When I was your age, I stood at this very place, just as lost as you are now. I, too, had a choice—to stay where life was safe or to step into the wild storm of possibility. And do you know what I realised?"*

Aryan shook his head.

Suraj's voice softened. *"The past is a comfortable prison. Many stay because it is familiar, not because it is right. But not every journey is an* escape, Aryan. Some are a calling—a whisper from the future, daring you to chase it."

The words stirred something deep within Aryan. The weight on his chest lessened, as if the old man had loosened the chains that held him back.

Suraj stood, his gaze steady. "If you stay, you will have a life. A good one, even. But will you ever look at the stars without wondering what lies beyond them? Will you ever walk these streets without asking, 'What if?'"

Aryan's heart pounded.

No. He did not want to live with *what-ifs*. He did not want to grow old, sitting at this very well, telling some younger man about the dreams he never chased.

He turned back to the road ahead.

Perhaps the journey was not an escape at all.

Perhaps it was an invitation—to become something more than he had ever imagined.

And so, he took his first step into destiny.

PART TWO

Love, Loss, and Learning

"The journey is never about reaching the treasure—it is about becoming the one who no longer needs it."

- Shree Shambav

CHAPTER III

The Unseen Power of Love

"True love does not ask you to choose between yourself and another. It walks beside you, not ahead or behind. It does not bind—it sets you free."

— Shree Shambav

The Unseen Power of Love

The world before him stretched vast and untamed, but his mind lingered on what he had left behind. The further he walked, the lighter his feet felt—yet the weight on his heart grew heavier.

Then, just as he reached the bend in the road, he heard a voice. Soft, yet unwavering.

"Aryan."

He turned.

She stood at the edge of the path, her long braid slipping over her shoulder like a ribbon of dusk. Meera. The girl who had watched him dream when the rest of the world called him foolish. The girl whose laughter had been his refuge on storm-heavy days.

For a long moment, neither spoke. The wind carried the scent of wet earth and blooming jasmine, a cruel reminder of home when he had already chosen to leave it.

She stepped forward. "So you're truly leaving?"

Aryan clenched his fists. "I have to, Meera. There's something out there waiting for me."

She tilted her head, studying him with the quiet intensity that always made him uneasy. "And you think you won't find it here?"

He exhaled sharply. "I know I won't. I need to become someone. To find my purpose. To—"

"To chase a dream that has never let you sleep," she finished, her voice holding neither mockery nor bitterness—only understanding.

He looked away. "I thought you, of all people, would understand."

"I do," she said softly. "That's why I'm here."

The wind tugged at her shawl as she looked down, as if searching for the right words among the dust and scattered leaves.

"Aryan, I won't ask you to stay. But before you go, answer me this—do you know what you're leaving behind?"

He frowned. "Of course I do."

"No," she said, stepping closer. "You know what you're going toward. But do you know what you're turning away from?"

Silence.

"Ambition is a fire," she continued, her voice as gentle as the breeze, yet edged with something he couldn't name. "It can warm you, or it can burn everything you love to ashes. And love… love is the rain. It can nourish the fire, make it stronger. But if you let it, it can also put it out."

Aryan swallowed hard. "So you're saying I have to choose?"

Meera held his gaze, her dark eyes searching his for answers even he didn't have. "No. I'm saying you need to understand that love and ambition don't always pull in the same direction."

The words struck him deeper than he expected. Could he chase greatness without leaving love behind? Could he reach for the unknown without losing what was familiar?

He wanted to tell her he would return, that no matter how far he went, he would find his way back. But even as the words formed in his throat, he realised how fragile they were—promises made at the crossroads of fate, easily lost in the winds of time.

Meera stepped back, the distance between them growing with each heartbeat. "Just remember," she said, "a man who walks too fast toward the future might outrun the things that truly matter."

Aryan nodded, though his heart felt heavier than before.

And then, without another word, he turned and walked away.

The road stretched on, the horizon waiting. But as he took each step, a question followed him, whispered in the voice of the girl he left behind:

Does love make us stronger by anchoring us, or weaker by making us vulnerable?

The Unseen Power of Love: The Crossroads of the Heart

The road stretched ahead, endless and uncertain, yet Aryan's steps slowed as though the weight of an unseen force anchored him. He had left behind his home, his village, his past—but Meera's words clung to him, echoing in the silence.

"A man who walks too fast toward the future might outrun the things that truly matter."

His grip tightened around the strap of his satchel. What if she was right? What if, in his pursuit of greatness, he was leaving behind something far more precious than gold, power, or fame?

Ahead, the dusty path led toward the unknown, filled with endless possibilities. But behind him, standing like a lone figure in the storm, was the one thing he had ever known for certain.

He turned back.

Meera was still there, standing at the edge of the path, her arms wrapped around herself as though shielding against the wind. She had not moved—not forward, not away. Just there. Waiting.

Aryan swallowed hard and walked back toward her, each step an unspoken battle between pride and longing. When he reached her, she looked up, her eyes unreadable.

"Still here?" she asked, her voice quiet but unwavering.

"So are you."

She smiled, but it was a sad kind of smile. "Maybe we're both waiting for something."

Aryan sighed and ran a hand through his hair. "Meera... I don't want to leave you behind. But I don't know how to stay either."

Her gaze softened. "Then maybe the question isn't whether you stay or leave. Maybe the question is—what is it that you're truly seeking?"

He exhaled. "I want to become something more. To prove to myself that I am more than just a boy with a dream."

Meera nodded, her fingers tracing invisible patterns in the dirt. "And you think love will hold you back?"

He hesitated. "Won't it?"

She studied him, then shook her head. "Love is not a chain, Aryan. It is the wind beneath your wings—if it is the right kind."

He frowned. "And how do we know the difference?"

Meera turned away slightly, her gaze drifting toward the horizon, as if the answer lay somewhere in the distance.

"The love that liberates," she said after a moment, "is the love that lets you grow, even if it means growing apart. It does not demand that you stay, nor does it fear your journey. It watches you go, and yet, it remains within you."

She turned back to him, her dark eyes steady. "But the love that limits? That is the love that asks you to shrink so that it can feel whole. It binds you with fear, with guilt, with the illusion that without it, you are nothing."

Aryan felt something stir deep within him, an ache that had no name.

"Which love do you think this is?" he asked, his voice barely above a whisper.

She smiled—a real smile this time, one that held no bitterness, only truth. "That is not for me to answer. That is for you to discover."

He stared at her, the weight of her words sinking into his chest like stones into a river.

Could love and ambition walk hand in hand? Could he chase his dreams without losing the ones who mattered?

And more than that—*could he ever truly succeed if he did not know how to love?*

Meera stepped closer, lifting her hand to his chest, right over his heart. "No matter where you go, Aryan… make sure you're not just running away. Make sure you're running toward something."

A lump formed in his throat. He wanted to say something—to tell her that he would return, that this was not goodbye, that love was not something he could afford to carry right now.

But as he looked into her eyes, he realised—love was never something to carry. It was something that carried *you*.

With a deep breath, he turned toward the road once more.

This time, as he walked away, he did not feel like he was leaving love behind.

He felt as if he was finally beginning to understand it.

CHAPTER IV

The Sacred Bond of Marriage

"Marriage is not the end of one's journey, but the birth of a shared path. It is not about losing oneself, but about growing into something greater—together."

— Shree Shambav

The Merchant's Wisdom and the Promise of Love

After months of relentless travel, Aryan arrived in the grand city of Taxila, where the air was thick with the scent of spices, ink, and ambition. This was a city where scholars debated in marble courtyards, traders bartered in bustling bazaars, and storytellers wove myths under ancient banyan trees. It was a place where destinies were shaped, where men came to seek knowledge, fortune, and sometimes, themselves.

With little money save for what his parents and his friend Rohan had given him, Aryan found himself drawn into the orbit of Rahim—a merchant of great wealth, greater wisdom, and an enigmatic past. Rahim was a man who could read a person's worth, not by their words but by their silence. He had built an empire of trade not merely through shrewdness, but through an uncanny understanding of human nature.

"You wish to learn the art of business?" Rahim had asked on their first meeting, his sharp eyes scanning Aryan's face like an old scroll.

Aryan had nodded, eager yet uncertain.

Rahim chuckled. "Business is not about gold or goods, boy. It is about knowing when to speak and when to listen."

Years passed under Rahim's mentorship. Aryan learned to measure the weight of silence in a negotiation, to see the stories etched in the hands of craftsmen, to understand that the true currency of trade was not silver, but trust. The marketplace became his teacher—the clamour of merchants haggling, the whispered conspiracies of traders plotting fortunes, the quiet understanding between a buyer and seller when a deal was fair.

Yet, amid the pursuit of wealth and wisdom, Aryan found his thoughts often drifting to love—not the fleeting infatuations of youth, but the kind that endured like an old melody. One evening, he witnessed a moment that would stay with him forever: a young couple, Zayd and Leila, standing under the moonlight, their hands intertwined as if the world beyond them did not exist.

They were not royalty. They owned no palaces. Their wealth lay in the quiet devotion in their eyes, in the way Zayd shielded Leila from the evening chill, in the way Leila smiled as if his presence alone was warmth enough. They reminded him of Meera—the woman he had left behind in his quest for destiny.

He had thought love could wait, that ambition was the more pressing call. But now, watching Zayd and Leila. The stars shimmered like scattered gold dust across the velvet sky as Aryan sat on the terrace of his palatial home in Taxila. The once-restless wanderer had become a man of means, his name spoken with respect among traders and merchants. Yet, as he gazed at the heavens, the wealth he had amassed felt weightless against the questions that now stirred within him.

Is marriage a union of two souls or the merging of two destinies?

The answer, he realised, was not simple. He had seen unions built on passion, only to fade like a fleeting summer breeze. He had witnessed marriages forged from duty, hollow and devoid of warmth. But then, there was Zayd and Leila—the young couple whose love had flourished despite trials and hardships. Their devotion was not merely the meeting of hearts but the weaving of two fates into a single thread, bound by something greater than either alone.

It was in their quiet moments, the way Leila's eyes searched for Zayd in a crowd, the way his fingers brushed against hers in reassurance, that Aryan saw the essence of true companionship. Love was not a fleeting emotion—it was a choice, made every day, to stand beside one another through storms and sunshine alike.

The marketplace had taught Aryan the art of negotiation, the power of persuasion, and the fragility of trust. But it was Rahim, his mentor, who had shown him something greater. The old merchant, once consumed by ambition, had spent his years accumulating riches, only to find himself alone in his twilight years.

He thought of Meera's laughter, of the way she had always challenged him, never content to let him live in his illusions. She had been his mirror, showing him both his strengths and his flaws. And now, for the first time in years, Aryan questioned whether chasing the horizon had been worth the distance he had placed between them.

The Final Lesson

As years passed, Rahim grew frail, his once sharp eyes dimming with time. He had no children of his own, and in Aryan, he saw not just a protégé but a son. One evening, as the sun dipped below the horizon, Rahim called Aryan to his bedside.

"Aryan," he whispered, his breath shallow, "I spent my life building wealth, believing it would bring me joy, that it would make me untouchable. I neglected my wife, dismissed love as a distraction. When she fell ill, I was too occupied with my trade routes, my ambitions. And then, one day, she was gone."

His trembling hand reached for Aryan's. "I prayed to the Divine for forgiveness, for someone to care for me in my old age. And in you, my boy, He answered. You have been more than my own blood." His lips curled into a weak smile, a tear slipping down his wrinkled cheek. "I do not know how to thank you."

Aryan clasped Rahim's hand tighter. "You have already given me more than I ever asked for."

With a final sigh, Rahim closed his eyes, a quiet peace settling over his face.

As Aryan sat beside him, the weight of Rahim's words sank deep into his soul. Wealth could be amassed, power could be wielded, but love—love was the only treasure that endured beyond the reaches of time.

Aryan swallowed the lump in his throat. He had admired Rahim's wisdom in business, but here, in this quiet confession, was the most profound lesson of all.

How does commitment transform love from a fleeting emotion into an enduring bond?

Aryan saw it clearly now—love without commitment was like rain without roots. It touched the earth but did not stay. It was commitment that made love grow deep, that turned passion into something unbreakable. It was the promise, renewed daily, to choose another over and over again.

That night, Aryan wrote a letter. His hand trembled as he sealed it with wax, knowing that his words carried a promise of their own:

Meera, upon my return, I will make you my wife.

He had been a fool to believe that love and ambition could not coexist. He had once thought love was a cage, something that would tether him to one place. But watching Rahim die with regret in his heart, Aryan understood now:

Can true love exist without the willingness to surrender parts of oneself?

The answer lay in the sacrifices made for love—not in losing oneself, but in intertwining paths so that one's journey was no longer walked alone. It was not about giving up freedom, but about finding a greater freedom in shared purpose.

Rahim's final words haunted him as the old man took his last breath, a tear slipping down his wrinkled cheek. "You are more than my blood, Aryan. The Divine has sent you to be my redemption."

Is a life of freedom richer than a life of shared purpose?

Aryan closed his eyes and saw Meera's face. He had chosen freedom once, chasing the horizon as if it held all the answers. But what was freedom, if it meant coming home to an empty house? What was success if there was no one to share it with?

The wind carried whispers through the night, and for the first time, he understood.

Love was not a burden, nor a cage.

It was the road that led him home.

And with that truth burning in his heart, Aryan knew where his journey would lead him next.

CHAPTER V

Children: Our Greatest Teachers

"Fate does not shout—it whispers. Only those who are still enough to listen will hear where they are meant to go."

– Shree Shambav

The days after Rahim's passing felt heavier than Aryan had anticipated. The bustling marketplace no longer carried the same allure, and the grand walls of his palatial home felt suffocating rather than luxurious. Success had once been his greatest ambition, yet now, standing at the peak of it, he felt a strange emptiness.

One evening, while wandering through the narrow streets of Taxila, he met Joseph—a young boy with eyes full of mischief and a smile that never seemed to fade. Joseph had no home, no wealth, and yet, he carried the joy of a man who had everything.

One afternoon, as they sat under the shade of a banyan tree, Aryan found himself asking, "Joseph, child, how come you are so happy?"

Joseph grinned, tilting his head as if the answer was obvious. "Sir, I have nothing to lose, and I have nothing to worry about."

Aryan chuckled, amused by the simplicity of the response. But Joseph wasn't finished. His small fingers traced patterns in the dirt before he looked up again and asked, "Sir, can I ask you something?"

"Of course."

"What is more valuable—gold or kindness?"

Aryan burst into laughter. "Gold, of course! Gold builds empires, feeds families, and grants power."

Joseph simply nodded, as if tucking away the answer for another time. But that night, while Aryan sat alone on his terrace beneath the sprawling sky, he heard a whisper in the wind—a voice, soft yet insistent.

"What is more valuable—gold or kindness?"

The question haunted him. For all the wealth he had amassed, what had it truly given him? Could riches bring back Rahim? Could gold replace the love he had left behind in Mira's waiting heart? Could it make him whole?

Days passed, and Aryan found himself lost in thought, his once-clear ambitions clouded by new uncertainties. He pondered another question, one that unsettled him even more:

Do we raise children, or do they raise us?

Joseph had no title, no possessions, and yet, he had left Aryan with a question that burned deeper than any lesson in trade. What if true wisdom did not come from wealth or age, but from the innocence of those untainted by greed and fear?

Still troubled, Aryan sought out a wise old monk who lived a few streets away. He found the sage seated beneath a withering tree, his hands resting calmly on his lap, his eyes closed as though listening to something unseen.

"Master," Aryan said, kneeling before him. "Is true legacy measured in material wealth, or in the values we pass on?"

The monk opened his eyes, a knowing smile on his lips. "Tell me, Aryan—when Rahim left this world, what did he leave you?"

Aryan hesitated before answering, "He left me his business, his wealth, his home."

The monk nodded. "And yet, what do you remember of him?"

Aryan swallowed hard. He remembered the night Rahim had taken his last breath, the sorrow in his voice as he spoke of the love he had neglected. He remembered the regret that had lined his mentor's face—not over lost wealth, but over the love he had failed to nurture.

"I remember his regrets," Aryan admitted softly. "His lessons. His words."

The monk smiled. "Then tell me, did he leave you wealth—or wisdom?"

Aryan lowered his head. "Wisdom."

The monk's gaze was steady. "Then why do you still ask me if legacy is measured in wealth?"

Aryan let the silence settle around him, the weight of the monk's words sinking in. For years, he had pursued riches, believing them to be the key to fulfillment. Yet here, in the quiet wisdom of a child and an old monk, he saw the truth—legacy was not about what one owned but about what one imparted.

Taking a deep breath, Aryan voiced the last question that had haunted him for days. "Master, how does parenthood challenge and redefine our understanding of responsibility?"

The monk closed his eyes for a moment before answering. "A man who seeks only to build a life for himself walks a lonely road. But a man who nurtures others—who raises a child, teaches a student, guides a friend—he builds something greater than himself."

Aryan thought of Rahim, of his own father, of Mira, and of Joseph. Perhaps true wealth was not gold or land. Perhaps true wealth is the love, the lessons, and the kindness we leave behind in the hearts of others.

And for the first time in years, Aryan felt a new kind of purpose stirring within him—a purpose not tied to wealth, but to the kind of legacy he wished to leave behind.

The Journey into the Unknown

The night stretched before him, endless and unyielding, as Aryan sat by the dying embers of his small fire.

He had come so far, yet the destination remained elusive.

The treasure that had haunted his childhood dreams was no longer just a pursuit of wealth or glory. It had become something more—a question he could not silence, a calling he could not ignore.

But how did one find a place that existed only in whispers and old legends? Who could lead him there when even Rahim, with all his wealth and influence, had failed?

Aryan exhaled, watching the dust swirl beneath the moonlight. He had spent years preparing for this journey, but now that he stood at the precipice of the unknown, doubt clawed at his resolve.

"How long will this journey be?" The thought gnawed at him.

Would it take months? Years? Would he wander until his bones became part of the very sands he walked upon? Or was the treasure just a myth, a mirage that had lured countless seekers to their ruin?

He closed his eyes, trying to quiet the storm within.

Rahim had done everything in his power to help him. He had reached out to scholars, traders, and travelers from distant lands—each inquiry met with dead ends. Even the most learned men had only vague tales, fragmented and uncertain.

"Perhaps some things are meant to remain lost," Rahim had once said.

But Aryan had never believed that.

Somewhere, buried beneath time and secrecy, the treasure existed. And it wasn't just gold or jewels he sought—it was **truth**.

The truth of why it called to him. The truth of why it had been hidden.

He looked to the horizon, where the stars glowed like celestial lanterns lighting his path. Somewhere beyond those dunes, beyond the rivers and valleys he had yet to cross, the answer awaited him.

The journey would be long. Perhaps longer than he imagined.

But turning back now was impossible.

He had stepped forward into the unknown, and there was only one way left to go—**forward.**

PART THREE

The Rise to Power and Fame

"Power is not a throne one sits upon, but a storm one learns to stand within. The moment you believe you control it, it begins to control you."

- *Shree Shambav*

CHAPTER VI

Mastering Wealth and Influence

"True legacy is not written in wealth or power, but in the hearts we touch, the love we give, and the wisdom we leave behind."

— Shree Shambav

The Weight of Power

Years passed after Rahim's passing, and the boy who had once set out to chase treasure had become a man who held power in the palm of his hand. Aryan had mastered the art of trade, not just in goods, but in people, in influence, in the unspoken currencies that truly governed the world—loyalty, fear, and ambition.

Taxila, once a city of learning and trade, had become too small for him. His reputation grew like wildfire, spreading beyond borders, reaching the ears of noblemen, rulers, and eventually, the Sultan himself. The invitation had come not as a request, but as an inevitability. A merchant could be ignored, but a man with power—true power—could never be overlooked.

But what was power?

Was it the weight of gold in one's vaults? The number of men willing to bend the knee? The fear one could strike in the hearts of enemies?

These questions whispered to Aryan at night, long after the wine had been poured and the feast had ended, long after the echoes of silk-clad nobles had faded into the halls of his growing empire.

One evening, he sat in his chamber, the flickering light of an oil lamp casting long shadows. Opposite him sat an old man, his face weathered like parchment, his eyes holding the wisdom of time itself. This was **Rizwan**, a scholar who had once advised kings before retreating into obscurity. Aryan had sought him out, needing a voice untainted by ambition.

"Tell me, Rizwan," Aryan leaned forward, his fingers laced together. "What is true power?"

The old man smiled, the kind of smile that comes from knowing the answer is one the listener may not yet be ready to hear.

"You have traveled far, Aryan," he said, his voice slow, deliberate. "You have touched gold, commanded men, stood in places where only the mighty dare to walk. And yet, you ask me this?"

Aryan exhaled, running a hand through his hair. "Because I do not know if I own power or if power now owns me."

Rizwan chuckled softly. "Ah, now that is the right question." He picked up a small clay cup, filling it with water from a brass jug. "Do you know why water is the most powerful element, Aryan?"

The merchant frowned. "Because it gives life?"

"Yes," Rizwan nodded. "But also because it takes it away. Water wears down mountains, drowns the unprepared, and yet, it yields to the gentlest touch." He swirled the cup in his hand. "Power is like this—those who try to control it, clutch it too tightly, will one day find it slipping through their fingers."

Aryan looked into his own reflection in the cup. "Then what should one do? If wealth is fleeting, if power corrupts, what is left?"

Rizwan leaned forward, his eyes searching Aryan's. "Purpose."

The Crossroads of Ambition and Identity

That night, Aryan found sleep elusive. His mind churned with Rizwan's words. **Purpose.** What had his purpose been when he first set out from home? To chase treasure? To prove himself? To be more than the nameless boy who had watched others carve their names into history?

He had achieved everything he had once dreamed of. He had power, respect, and the ears of rulers. And yet, something was missing—something vital.

Mira's voice returned to him in memory, soft as the wind, yet as unyielding as the tide.

"Is a life of freedom richer than a life of shared purpose?"

He had once believed freedom was the ability to move unchained, to chase the horizon without looking back. But now, standing at the summit of everything he had ever wanted, he felt a strange emptiness—a realisation that no matter how much gold he gathered, how many men bowed before him, **the echoes of a life lived alone could never replace the warmth of one truly shared.**

He thought of Rahim's last words, of the regret hidden behind a life of success.

"I thought wealth would bring me joy, but I was wrong."

Would Aryan one day whisper the same in his final breath?

The Game of Shadows

Power came with its price. Influence was a blade—sharp, dangerous, and unpredictable. The Sultan's court was a battlefield of whispers, where alliances shifted like desert sand, where smiles masked daggers, and trust was a currency rarer than diamonds.

Aryan had spent years mastering trade, but this… this was different. **Here, a single misstep did not cost coin—it cost lives.**

He learned quickly. He played their game. But there was one question he could never answer—was he becoming the very kind of man he had once despised?

One night, he met **Azhar**, the Sultan's chief advisor, a man whose voice held more power than armies. Azhar studied Aryan with sharp eyes, a knowing smirk playing at his lips.

"You are not like the others," he mused.

Aryan frowned. "Is that a compliment or a warning?"

Azhar chuckled. "Both. You still believe in something, I can see it. That is dangerous."

"Belief is dangerous?"

"In a world of wolves, a man with a heart is either a king... or dead." Azhar leaned closer. "Tell me, Aryan—do you think you can wield power and still remain untouched by it?"

Aryan had no answer.

The Unfinished Question

Days passed. Weeks. Aryan stood before the Sultan, delivering reports, advising on trade routes, gaining favor. But at night, he sat in silence, listening to the whispers in his own heart.

"What is true power?"

"Is wealth merely a means to an end, or does it corrupt those who chase it?"

"Can a man hold power without losing himself?"

And above all, the one question he feared the most:

"If I had everything, but no one to share it with, would I truly have anything at all?"

The answers did not come easily. Perhaps they never would.

CHAPTER VII

The Art of Strategy

"Strategy can shape a battle, but it cannot command the hearts of men. The greatest victories are won not with the sword, but with trust."

— Shree Shambav

The Sultan's palace was a city within a city, a place where whispers held the weight of swords, and silence was often deadlier than war. Marble pillars lined the halls, their intricate carvings whispering stories of victories and betrayals. Aryan walked among them, not as a mere merchant, but as an advisor to power, a strategist whose words shaped the course of trade, diplomacy, and even war.

The Nature of Power

Power was not about gold, he had learned, nor was it about armies. It was about understanding men—their fears, their desires, and their weaknesses.

One evening, while standing on the terrace of the Sultan's court, he found himself in conversation with the Grand Vizier, Malik Zafar, a man whose face held more secrets than the archives of the kingdom.

"You have a sharp mind, Aryan," Malik remarked, swirling a goblet of wine in his hands. "But tell me—what is real power?"

Aryan did not answer immediately. Instead, he looked over the vast city, where torches flickered like stars against the endless darkness. "Power," he finally said, "is not held by those who are feared, nor by those who are loved. It is held by those who understand the minds of both."

Malik smiled. "Then you are learning well."

But Aryan wondered—was he becoming what he once despised? The Sultan's court was a chessboard, and he was now a player. Did he control the game, or was he just another piece moved by unseen hands?

The Art of Negotiation

One of Aryan's greatest tests came when he faced Farhad al-Rashid, a seasoned merchant whose monopoly over the spice trade had made him nearly untouchable. Farhad was a man who trusted only profit and saw kindness as a weakness.

Aryan met him in the Sultan's marketplace, where the scents of saffron and cinnamon mingled with the murmurs of merchants striking deals. "A man who controls the spices controls the taste of kings," Farhad said, his voice laced with arrogance.

Aryan simply smiled. "A man who controls the roads controls where the spices go."

Farhad's eyes narrowed. He had expected a merchant, not a tactician.

Aryan continued, "I have secured new routes through the northern passes. My men have made deals with tribes that will ensure no caravan crosses without my approval. Your monopoly is an illusion, Farhad. Partner with me, and we both prosper. Oppose me, and you will find your warehouses full, but your pockets empty."

Farhad studied him, then let out a slow laugh. "You play the game well, Aryan." He extended his hand. "Let us see how far we can take it."

Alliances and Betrayals

The Sultan's court was not a place of loyalty. It was a stage where alliances were masks worn until they were no longer needed. Aryan learned this when a trusted ally, Rashid Khan, a nobleman he had supported, turned against him.

Aryan sat in his chamber when a messenger arrived, breathless and pale. "My lord, Rashid has accused you of plotting against the Sultan."

A cold wave of realisation washed over Aryan. He had played his cards well, but he had underestimated how quickly a friend could become an enemy.

That night, Malik Zafar visited him. "You have two choices," the Vizier said. "Flee and be branded a traitor. Or stay, fight, and prove you are smarter than your enemies."

Aryan clenched his fists. He had come too far to let another man write his fate. He did not need to run; he needed to outmanoeuvre.

Personal Growth

The accusations did not break Aryan. They refined him.

He uncovered Rashid's corruption, bringing evidence before the Sultan himself. When the trial ended, Rashid was exiled, and the Aryan's influence grew stronger. But with every victory, a question gnawed at him—was this truly who he wanted to be?

One night, standing alone in the garden, he whispered to the stars, "I have everything I once dreamed of, yet why does my soul feel restless?"

Perhaps power was not the answer. Perhaps something deeper, something more enduring, awaited him beyond the games of the court.

And so, the strategist, the merchant, the man who had risen from nothing, found himself facing a question more difficult than any trade deal or battle:

What was the price of the path he had chosen—and was he willing to pay it?

CHAPTER VIII

The Gift of Giving

"A hand that gives is never empty, for generosity is the only treasure that multiplies when shared."

– Shree Shambav

The Burden of Gold

The night was silent, yet the weight on Aryan's soul was deafening. His chamber, adorned with silks and gold, felt emptier than ever. He had amassed riches beyond his dreams, earned the favour of the powerful, and built an empire stretching across lands, yet something within him remained unsatisfied.

He stood on the balcony of his grand residence, gazing at the stars that seemed so distant, so indifferent to the affairs of men. A memory surfaced—the laughter of a boy, innocent and free.

Joseph, a street child with nothing, yet richer than the wealthiest merchants Aryan had known.

"What is more valuable—gold or kindness?" the boy had once asked, his face glowing with a wisdom far beyond his years.

Aryan had laughed then, dismissing it as the question of a child who had never known true power. But now, years later, with all the gold and power in his grasp, the question returned, whispering through the corridors of his restless mind.

That night, he drifted into sleep with the question lingering in his heart.

The Man in Rags

The next morning, as Aryan's palanquin moved through the bustling streets of Taxila, he ordered it to halt. Something had caught his eye—a man, dressed in torn and ragged clothes, kneeling beside another man who could barely walk.

The beggar—no, the giver—was helping the disabled man to his feet, dusting off his tattered shawl, speaking to him with warmth and kindness. There was something radiant about his face, something peaceful, as though he carried no burdens, though his condition suggested otherwise.

Aryan watched in silence. The man had nothing, yet he gave freely.

For a long moment, Aryan remained rooted to the spot. Finally, he stepped forward.

"You struggle to meet your own needs," Aryan said, his voice edged with curiosity. "Why do you help others?"

The man turned to him, his smile gentle, his eyes filled with something Aryan could not name—perhaps clarity, perhaps something more.

"Because what I have is meant to be shared," the man replied. "Kindness is not a burden; it is the only wealth that grows the more you give it."

Aryan hesitated. "Can I help you?"

The man chuckled softly, shaking his head. "You can help many. But first, you must ask yourself—do you wish to give, or do you wish to trade?"

Before Aryan could respond, the man disappeared into the crowd, leaving only his words behind.

The Measure of Wealth

Aryan stood there, unmoving, lost in thought.

Was wealth measured by possessions or by the impact one left on others?

He had spent his life accumulating, believing power came from having more. But what if true power lay in giving away, in creating rather than hoarding?

Was generosity a sacrifice, or was it the only real investment?

That evening, Aryan called Joseph to his chamber. The boy, now older, stood before him, his eyes still filled with the same brightness Aryan had once dismissed as mere innocence.

Aryan placed a pouch of gold in his hands. "Go home," he said, his voice steady yet soft. "Go where your heart has always belonged."

Joseph looked up at him, hesitant. "But sir… why?"

Aryan exhaled slowly. "Because I finally understand what you meant, all those years ago."

The boy's face broke into a wide smile, and at that moment, Aryan felt something shift within him. It was not a loss. It was not a sacrifice.

It was freedom.

For the first time in years, he felt weightless.

And in that moment, he realised—perhaps Joseph had been his greatest teacher all along.

CHAPTER IX

Indulgence and Its Illusions

"We wander far in search of treasures, only to realise that what we long for was never beyond us, but within."

— Shree Shambav

The palace was filled with light and laughter, music drifting through the halls like a river that never ran dry. Aryan sat at the banquet table, his fingers brushing over the golden goblet in front of him, its jeweled rim catching the flickering glow of countless lamps. Around him, nobles raised their voices in drunken merriment, toasting to their victories, their wealth, their endless pleasures.

But Aryan felt nothing. The wine had lost its taste. The silken robes draping his frame were no warmer than the simple cotton tunic he had worn as a boy. The riches before him—glistening fruits, spiced meats, rare wines—felt like dust on his tongue.

He closed his eyes. Somewhere, far from this palace, there was the scent of freshly baked bread, the warmth of the sun rising over his childhood home, and the laughter of Rohan echoing through the narrow village streets. *When will I find my treasure? When will I be back home?*

That night, as he lay beneath a sky full of stars, a question whispered through his mind:

"When does enjoyment turn into excess, and fulfilment into emptiness?"

The next morning, burdened by thoughts he could not escape, Aryan wandered the city streets until he came upon a quiet courtyard. There, seated on a simple mat, was Yusuf, a wise ascetic draped in humble robes, his presence radiating a stillness that felt untouched by time.

Aryan sat before him, hesitant at first, before speaking the question that had haunted him. "When does enjoyment turn into excess, and fulfilment into emptiness?"

Yusuf smiled, his eyes holding the weight of countless years. "Enjoyment is like the rain—it nourishes when it comes in its time. But when it pours without end, it drowns the land."

Aryan listened, the words settling into the cracks of his soul. "Can we ever truly satisfy desires, or do they simply grow in new forms?"

The old man chuckled softly, shaking his head. "Desires, when fed without restraint, only grow hungrier. A man who chases pleasure will find it always running ahead of him."

Aryan frowned, his fingers tightening around the hilt of his dagger. He had spent years believing that wealth and indulgence would bring him happiness. But each new possession, each new pleasure, had only left him thirsting for more.

"Then tell me, Yusuf," he said, his voice quieter now. "Is self-control a form of deprivation, or is it the highest form of freedom?"

Yusuf's gaze softened. "A man who is a slave to his desires believes self-control is a prison. But a man who has tamed his desires knows it is the key that unlocks every chain."

Aryan fell silent.

The feasts, the luxuries, the intoxicating thrill of power—they had all been distractions. They had numbed the ache in his heart, but they had not healed it. He had mistaken indulgence for joy, and now, he wondered if he had spent years drinking from a cup that could never be filled.

One final question lingered on his lips. "Does indulgence bring joy, or is it just a temporary escape from emptiness?"

Yusuf looked up at the sky. "Pleasure is like a mirage—it offers a glimpse of water, but leaves you thirstier with each step toward it. True joy, Aryan, is not found in what you take in, but in what you give away."

Aryan's breath caught in his throat.

Aryan's Realisation

The weight of Yusuf's words settled over Aryan like the hush of dawn after a long storm. He felt as if he had been walking in a desert, chasing a shimmering mirage, only to realise that the oasis had never been there.

His mind drifted back to the countless nights he had spent in his palatial home, surrounded by gold and silk, yet feeling emptier than the beggar on the street. He thought of Rahim, a man who had amassed wealth beyond measure yet, in his final moments, had found solace not in riches but in Aryan's companionship.

"Pleasure is like a mirage—it offers a glimpse of water but leaves you thirstier with each step toward it."

Yusuf's words repeated in his mind, each syllable peeling away a layer of illusion.

Aryan had once believed wealth would bring security, that indulgence would bring joy, that power would bring fulfilment. But what had he gained? A house grand enough to echo with emptiness. A reputation built on admiration and fear rather than love. A life filled with feasts yet starved of meaning.

For the first time, he saw the faces of those he had left behind not as memories but as fragments of himself—pieces he had abandoned in his pursuit of something greater, only to realise he had been running in the wrong direction.

He thought of Joseph, the street boy who had smiled so freely despite owning nothing.

"Sir, I have nothing to lose, and I have nothing to worry about."

He thought of the poor man on the street, helping another despite his struggles.

"Just share what you have, and you will know the truth."

He thought of the aroma of fresh bread, of rain-soaked earth, of laughter shared in simpler days.

"Perhaps true wealth was never meant to be counted in coins, but in moments."

Aryan exhaled, feeling something shift within him. It was as if a heavy chain had been removed from around his chest—a chain he hadn't even known he was carrying.

He turned to Yusuf, his voice quieter but steadier than before. "Then what is the path to true fulfilment, if not through indulgence?"

The old man smiled. "Gratitude, service, and love."

Aryan nodded, understanding now what had been missing all along.

Perhaps the treasure he had been searching for was never gold, nor power, nor indulgence.

Perhaps it had been something else all along.

CHAPTER X

The Dance of Joy and Sorrow

"Joy and sorrow walk hand in hand; to know one is to embrace the other. Only those who welcome both truly understand life."

— Shree Shambav

Aryan stood by the balcony of his grand estate, overlooking the city that bore his name in whispers—some with admiration, others with envy. The night was alive with music and laughter from his courtyards, where merchants, nobles, and foreign emissaries celebrated another successful trade deal. Yet, despite the grandeur, his heart felt like a vacant temple—echoing with silence.

He turned his gaze upward. The moon, half-veiled by drifting clouds, reminded him of something his father had once said: *"The moon waxes and wanes, my son, but it is always whole. So too is life—joy and sorrow are but its changing faces."*

A knock on the door pulled him from his reverie. It was Yusuf, the ascetic he had met months ago.

"You did not join the celebration," Yusuf observed, stepping forward, his robes simple yet carrying an air of dignity.

Aryan exhaled. "Is it strange that I find no joy in my own victories?"

Yusuf smiled, taking a seat beside him. "Not strange, but revealing."

Aryan furrowed his brow. "I have everything I once desired. Wealth. Recognition. A name that echoes beyond lands I have yet to see. And yet..." His voice trailed off as he turned back to the distant stars.

"You feel a void," Yusuf completed his thought.

Aryan nodded. "I used to believe happiness was a destination. That once I reached it, I would remain there. But each triumph has demanded a sacrifice. Each joy has been followed by sorrow. I celebrated my rise in trade, yet I wept when Rahim left this world. I built a home grander than any in my village, yet it lacks the warmth of my childhood home. I have gained the world, but at what cost?"

Yusuf listened, then said, "Tell me, Aryan, can we truly appreciate joy without having known sorrow?"

Aryan thought of the day Rahim had died—the sorrow that had clutched his heart. He recalled the time he had lost Mira, not to death, but to the choices he had made. And then, he thought of the moments of joy—the exhilaration of his first successful negotiation, the laughter shared with Rohan, the warmth of his mother's embrace when he was young. Would those joys have been as sweet without the contrast of his pain?

"I suppose not," he admitted. "But then, why do we chase happiness when peace is more enduring?"

Yusuf chuckled. "Because happiness is a moment, a spark. It excites us, gives us a reason to move forward. But peace—peace is a river. It does not flash like fire, but it sustains. Few seek it, because it does not dazzle like gold. But those who find it..." He looked at Aryan meaningfully. "They do not hunger anymore."

Aryan remained silent for a while, absorbing his words. "How do we learn to embrace both the highs and lows of life? How do we not resist sorrow when it comes?"

Yusuf placed a gentle hand on Aryan's shoulder. "By understanding that both are necessary. The tree that basks in the sun must also endure the storm. The ocean that glistens in the morning light must also weather the tempest. Sorrow is not your enemy, Aryan. It is your teacher."

Aryan lowered his gaze. "Then suffering... is not a curse?"

"It is the gateway to deeper understanding," Yusuf answered. "You have spent your life conquering lands, wealth, and power. But the greatest conquest, Aryan, is the one within."

A silence stretched between them, but it was not empty. It was filled with something new—an understanding the Aryan had not possessed before. Perhaps life was not about avoiding sorrow but learning to dance with both joy and pain, to accept them as twin companions on the road.

And for the first time in years, Aryan did not feel lost. He felt... whole.

CHAPTER XI

The Weight of Walls

"A man builds walls to shelter himself from the world, only to realise they have become his prison."

— Shree Shambav

Aryan sat in his grand chair, staring at the vast emptiness of his palatial home. The walls, adorned with intricate carvings and tapestries from distant lands, whispered stories of wealth, triumph, and power. Yet, amidst all this magnificence, he felt a hollowness creeping into his soul.

His fingers idly traced the rim of an untouched goblet, his thoughts drifting to a distant past—the scent of rain-kissed earth, the sound of laughter echoing through the village fields, the warmth of stolen mangoes shared with Suraj beneath the banyan tree.

He closed his eyes and let the memory unfold.

"I will build a grand home one day," Aryan had declared, his young voice bursting with the certainty of an untested dream. "A place so vast, no one will ever call me poor again."

Suraj laughed, shaking his head. "A house does not make a man rich, Aryan."

Decades had passed. Time, like an invisible sculptor, had chiselled away his youth, yet the echoes of those words still lingered.

That evening, as the golden sun bathed the city in its dying light, Aryan welcomed Peter, his old friend, into his vast estate. They had started as merchants together in Taxila, but their paths had diverged—Aryan had risen to power, and Peter had remained a simple trader.

Peter stepped into the grand hall, his eyes scanning the towering walls, the shimmering chandeliers, and the corridors that seemed to stretch endlessly.

"This house..." Aryan murmured, more to himself than to Peter. "It was supposed to be everything."

Peter met his gaze. "And is it?"

Aryan hesitated. Then, with a wry chuckle, he answered, "I built these walls to keep the world out, Peter. But perhaps I only succeeded in trapping myself within them."

They wandered the silent halls together. Aryan pointed to his collection of rare antiques, his gold-plated shelves, his silk-draped chambers. But there was no pride in his voice—only detachment.

Peter stopped before a grand painting of Aryan, draped in opulent robes, his face carved with the weight of ambition. He turned to Aryan. "Do you remember the night we slept under the banyan tree?"

Aryan smiled faintly. "The stars looked so close, we thought we could catch them in our palms."

Peter nodded. "You said the sky was the greatest roof a man could have."

Aryan exhaled, running a hand through his greying hair. "And yet, here I am, beneath a roof of gold, missing a sky that was once mine."

His words sat between them like an uninvited guest. And in that silence, four questions whispered through the corridors of his heart—questions he had long ignored but could no longer escape.

Does a grand home bring security, or does it trap us in illusions of permanence?

Aryan turned to the towering walls, unyielding and impenetrable. Yet, could they guard against the loneliness that crept in through every unspoken moment, every absent voice? Could they keep time from stealing the things that truly mattered?

What makes a house a home—its size or the love within it?

This house had space for a hundred, but not one soul who truly understood him. He had built doors wide enough to welcome kings, but no threshold that led him back to Meera's embrace. What good were walls if the warmth that made them a home had long since faded?

Can wealth ever replace the richness of human connection?

He had spent years gathering riches, stacking them like bricks to build his empire. But in that vast, empty home, he found no comfort in gold, no laughter in silver, no solace in silk. Wealth had given him everything—except what his heart had once cherished the most.

Are the walls we build meant to keep others out or to keep ourselves in?

Perhaps he had not built his home as a sanctuary but as a fortress. A fortress to protect himself from loss, from vulnerability, from the ghosts of his past. But now, he saw the truth—these walls did not shield him; they caged him. And outside them, life had moved on without him.

Peter's voice was gentle. "It is not too late, Aryan."

Aryan looked at his old friend, searching his face for some answer, some direction. "Then tell me, Peter. What do I do?"

Peter smiled. "Perhaps it is time to open the doors."

That night, as the oil lamps flickered and the wind whispered through the cold halls, Aryan made a silent promise—to himself, to the ghosts of his past, to the love he had lost. He would seek his true treasure, not in wealth, but in something far greater.

Yet his treasure hunt remained a question.

CHAPTER XII

The Illusion of Control

"The more we seek to control, the more we become prisoners of our own desires. True power is not in holding, but in knowing when to let go."

– Shree Shambav

The halls of the Sultan's palace were never silent. Even in the stillness of night, whispers slithered through the corridors—words woven with ambition, deceit, and fear. Aryan had walked these halls for years, his presence commanding respect, his counsel shaping the empire's future. He had become more than a merchant; he was a kingmaker, a master of influence, a strategist whose words carried the weight of gold.

And yet, as he stood at the edge of the palace balcony, overlooking the city bathed in the dim glow of lanterns, he felt something unsettling in his chest. The restlessness he had once known as a boy, the hunger for more, had not disappeared. It had only changed its form.

Once, he had longed for wealth. Then, for power. And now—now, he wasn't sure what he longed for at all.

Is power a path to freedom or another kind of prison?

Aryan had spent a lifetime chasing power, believing it would grant him control over his fate. But the more influence he wielded, the more he saw its chains. The Sultan, for all his wealth, could not move without a hundred eyes watching him. His ministers, for all their knowledge, lived in fear of a single misplaced word. Even Aryan himself, once a free-spirited trader, now measured every step, every breath, with caution.

He had witnessed rulers crushed beneath the weight of their own thrones, their crowns too heavy with expectation. He had seen ministers who spoke in riddles, afraid to utter a truth that could cost them their lives. He had seen men who controlled armies, only to be prisoners of their paranoia.

Where was the freedom in power?

Where was the peace in control?

And was he, too, now nothing more than another pawn in a grander game?

Does controlling others mean we have control over ourselves?

Aryan had once believed that mastery over others meant mastery over himself. He had studied the art of persuasion, learned the dance of politics, and built alliances with the precision of a weaver threading silk. And yet, here he was— haunted by sleepless nights, weighed down by a hollowness that power could not fill.

One evening, he watched as the Sultan dined alone, surrounded by riches, yet utterly isolated. The most powerful man in the empire, and yet, he could not even trust the food on his plate without a servant tasting it first.

Aryan had everything, yet something within him whispered that he had lost himself along the way.

Was he truly in control of his life, or was he merely a man playing a role written for him by his own ambition?

When we seek to control the world, do we lose ourselves in the process?

There was a time when Aryan had dreams—simple dreams of love, of freedom, of returning home. But power had a way of changing people, of reshaping their desires until they no longer recognised their own hearts.

He thought of Meera. Her laughter had once been the melody of his life. But now, it had been years since he had heard it.

He thought of Suraj, of the village, of the endless sky they had once run beneath. He had traded all of it for golden palaces, for the company of men who smiled with daggers behind their backs.

What had he truly gained?

What had he lost?

Is the pursuit of control an illusion, leading us further from what truly matters?

One night, Aryan stood at the palace gates, watching a beggar boy chase fireflies under the moonlight. The child had nothing—no wealth, no status, no name of importance. And yet, he was free in a way Aryan had not been in years.

At that moment, something inside him cracked.

He had spent his life trying to master the world, only to become a prisoner of the very power he had sought.

The illusion of control had bound him tighter than any chains ever could.

For true freedom was never found in controlling the world— it was in letting go of the need to.

CHAPTER XIII

Beyond the Fabric of Identity

"A man draped in silk may still shiver in the cold, while a beggar wrapped in rags may carry the warmth of a thousand suns."

— Shree Shambav

The night was heavy with rain, the kind that drowned the sounds of the city in a ceaseless murmur. Aryan stood by his open window, watching the droplets race down the glass. The cool air carried the scent of damp earth and memories—memories of a night long past.

He closed his eyes, and suddenly, he was back on that treacherous road, the weight of gold-heavy bags strapped to his horse, Rahim's words echoing in his ears:

"Aryan, these are precious goods. Handle them personally."

It had been a simple task—travel to the nearby city, make the trade, and return before sundown. But fate, as always, had other plans.

The Ambush

Aryan had cleared his dealings before noon, his negotiation skills slicing through bargains like a master swordsman. But the return journey took an unexpected turn when the rains came, washing away paths and forcing them onto a lesser-known route. The terrain was rough, dense with trees that whispered secrets to the wind. The road was feared for one reason—robbers.

Halfway through, shadows emerged from the trees, swift and ruthless. A band of men, their faces masked, their knives glinting in the dimming light. Aryan and his men fought back, but they were outnumbered. The bandits stripped them of everything—some coins, horses, even the clothes on their backs.

Left with nothing but exhaustion and a bruised sense of pride, Aryan and his men wandered through the forest, the darkness thick and unforgiving.

Then, a flicker of hope.

A small lamp glowed atop a distant hill.

The Refuge on the Hill

Weary and shivering, Aryan knocked on the wooden door. It creaked open to reveal an old man, his back curved like a crescent moon, leaning on a stick. Beside him, an elderly woman, her eyes filled with the kindness of a thousand forgotten stories.

She smiled. "Come in, son. You must be cold."

Before Aryan could speak, she handed him a bundle of dry clothes. The warmth of the fabric against his skin was more comforting than he could have imagined. A hot herbal tea followed, its aroma wrapping around him like an embrace.

As they sat by the crackling fire, the old man finally spoke. *"You can rest here for the night. The roads are unkind after dark."*

Aryan wanted to refuse, but fatigue made the choice for him.

By dawn, the first rays of sunlight painted the sky in soft hues of gold and crimson. Aryan stepped outside, inhaling the scent of blooming flowers, damp earth, and fresh tea. Butterflies danced over the garden, bees hummed in quiet labour. There was no wealth here—no silks, no gold, no treasures. And yet, Aryan had never felt richer.

"I have lost everything, and yet, I feel lighter," he murmured.

The old woman, overhearing, chuckled. "Perhaps you've lost nothing at all."

Before leaving, Aryan turned to them. "Come with me. Be my guests. I would be honoured to host you."

The old man smiled, shaking his head. "This is our home, child. We are happy here."

Something in their voices stayed with Aryan as he made his way back to the city.

The Merchant's Door

Hours later, their feet burned against the hot ground as they approached the city gates. Parched and exhausted, they stopped at the house of a wealthy merchant. Aryan, still dressed in the simple tunic the old couple had given him, called out, *"Water, please. Just a little for our thirst."*

The merchant took one look at their worn clothes and sunburnt faces before curling his lips in disdain. *"Guards, remove these beggars."*

The doors slammed shut.

For the first time, Aryan tasted the bitterness of being unseen. The weight of wealth had never denied him dignity, but the lack of it now made him invisible.

That night, standing on the terrace, the city lights below him like fallen stars, Aryan felt the wind whisper through his thoughts.

That night, as the rain drummed against his terrace, Aryan felt his mind slip into a restless storm. The past few days had unsettled him, shaking the foundation upon which he had built his life. His encounter with the old couple and the merchant had left him questioning everything he had once taken for granted.

He exhaled slowly, watching the flickering city lights below. The golden palaces, the bustling markets, the riches stacked behind walls—none of it felt as real as the warmth of the fire in the old couple's hut.

The wind carried his thoughts into the vast night, whispering his questions back to him.

Do the clothes we wear define who we are, or do they conceal our truth?

The old woman's face came to his mind—the kindness in her wrinkled smile, the gentleness with which she had offered him dry clothes. She hadn't cared that he arrived at her door robbed, drenched, and helpless. She had seen only a weary traveller, not a ruined merchant.

But the merchant in the city? He had seen only the rags.

When Aryan stood before the merchant's gates, stripped of his usual silks and jewels, he had been turned away without a second glance. Was he no longer the same Aryan simply because his garments had changed?

"If clothes can make a man powerful, can they also make him powerless?" he wondered aloud.

For years, he had wrapped himself in the finest fabrics, believing they were symbols of his success. But now he saw them for what they truly were—costumes in a grand illusion, a disguise that determined how the world treated him.

Perhaps, in shedding his silks, he had come closer to seeing himself.

How much of our identity is shaped by external appearances?

He remembered how, in his youth, he had idolised the wealthy traders who walked through the bustling streets of his village. Their robes shimmered in the sun, their perfumes left trails of power behind them.

"This is success," he had told himself. "This is what I must become."

And he had.

But in that moment outside the merchant's door, his wealth had disappeared—not because it was truly gone, but because it could no longer be seen.

Did identity shift so easily? Was he the same Aryan, or had the world rewritten his worth based on his appearance?

The old couple had seen him as a human being, nothing more and nothing less. But the merchant had seen only what his eyes allowed—a beggar unworthy of even a cup of water.

Was the world so blind? Or had he been blind all along?

Can we ever be truly seen if we are afraid to be vulnerable?

Aryan had spent his life fortifying himself—against weakness, against failure, against the kind of poverty he had once known. He had built his fortune with the precision of a man carving a statue, carefully chiselling away his old self, refining an image of power and control.

But had he ever allowed anyone to see the raw stone beneath?

Had he ever let anyone see the Aryan who still longed for simple joys—the smell of rain-soaked earth, the taste of freshly baked bread, the laughter of his childhood friend Suraj?

He had hidden that part of himself so well, even he had forgotten it.

But the old woman had not needed his wealth to welcome him. She had not needed proof of his importance. She had simply seen a tired man in need of shelter.

And perhaps, that was the deepest kind of seeing—the kind that had nothing to do with power, wealth, or appearances.

Is freedom found in presenting an image or in shedding all facades?

Aryan closed his eyes and saw himself standing before a mirror, dressed in his finest robes, adorned with jewels, holding the world's respect in his hands.

Then, he saw himself stripped of all of it—standing in the old couple's humble home, wearing simple cloth, drinking tea by the fire.

Which version of himself was truly free?

The version bound by expectations, by titles, by the constant need to uphold an image?

Or the one who had nothing to prove, who had been welcomed as a mere man, not as a merchant, not as a powerful figure, but simply as Aryan?

The wind howled, and he heard the truth in its voice.

Freedom was not in how the world saw him. It was in how he saw himself.

Aryan's Awakening

As the storm settled, so did Aryan's heart.

He thought of the old couple's home—a place with no treasures, yet rich beyond measure. He thought of the merchant's grand estate, filled with gold, yet empty of kindness.

For years, he had chased wealth, believing it would make him untouchable. But tonight, as he stood alone in his grand chamber, he realised—

Wealth does not make a man untouchable. It only makes him forget what it means to be truly seen.

PART FOUR

The Truths We Resist

"In the quiet spaces of the heart, where the noise of the world fades, the soul whispers truths that words cannot express."

-Shree Shambav

CHAPTER XIV

The Cost of Power

"A man in power must choose: to be feared or to be trusted. But fear is a blade that cuts both ways, and trust is a bridge that, once burned, may never be rebuilt. To have both is an illusion, and to have neither is to stand alone in a kingdom of shadows."

— Shree Shambav

The grand halls of Aryan's estate were lined with the finest tapestries, the air thick with the scent of burning incense and the whispers of those who sought his favor. Ministers, merchants, and noblemen bowed before him, their words drenched in flattery. But in their eyes, he saw something else—calculation, hunger, fear.

Power had once seemed like a crown of gold, but now, it felt more like chains.

One evening, Aryan stood on his balcony, looking out at the city below. He had built an empire from nothing. Yet, as he gazed at the streets, he could not shake the emptiness gnawing at his soul.

His oldest advisor, Omar, stepped beside him. "You have everything a man could dream of," Omar said, his voice gentle yet firm. "Why do you look so troubled?"

Aryan let out a hollow laugh. "Everything, Omar? Or nothing at all?"

Omar studied him carefully. "You are feared. Respected. Even kings seek your wisdom. Is that not what you wanted?"

Aryan's grip tightened on the balcony railing. "I wanted security, Omar. I wanted never to feel powerless again. But tell me, at what cost? I have seen those closest to me betray me for gold. I have watched trust dissolve like salt in water. I have gained the world but lost the simplicity of love, of friendship, of peace."

Omar sighed, placing a hand on Aryan's shoulder. "Power does not change men, Aryan. It reveals them. If you have lost something, it was never because you gained power, but because you chose which parts of yourself to silence along the way."

Aryan turned to face him. "Then tell me, old friend, is power a gift or a curse?"

Omar smiled sadly. "It is neither. It is a test. And few pass it without losing themselves."

That night, Aryan lay awake, staring at the intricate patterns of his ceiling, carved by the finest artisans. But no carving, no gold, no wealth could fill the hollow space within him.

He thought of his younger self—running barefoot through the fields, laughing with Rohan, listening to his mother's lullabies. He had traded all of that for power. But had he won, or had he lost?

Four questions burned in his mind, their weight pressing against his chest like an invisible force:

1. Does power grant freedom, or does it shackle us in the very ambitions we once thought would liberate us?
2. Can power and trust ever walk hand in hand, or does one always come at the cost of the other?
3. Does influence bring fulfillment, or does it merely sharpen the hunger for more, leaving the soul emptier with each conquest?
4. When does ambition cease to be a guiding force and transform into an unquenchable thirst that consumes everything in its path?

That night, as exhaustion finally pulled Aryan into sleep, his restless mind wove a dream. But this was no ordinary dream—it was an answer. The four questions, like specters, stood before him, whispering their truths.

CHAPTER XV

Justice Beyond Revenge

"True justice is not found in the letters of law, but in the spaces between them. It is not measured in punishment, but in the mercy we dare to show."

— Shree Shambav

The night air carried the scent of burning oil lamps as Aryan stood on the terrace of his grand estate, staring into the horizon. The city below was alive with whispers of justice and vengeance—two forces that had shaped his journey in ways he could no longer ignore.

The Weight of Betrayal

The night of Faizan's betrayal was one Aryan could never forget. The scent of rain-drenched earth still clung to his memory, the same way the ache of betrayal never truly left his soul. The city streets had been alive that evening—markets filled with laughter, merchants shouting their final bargains before closing their stalls, the scent of freshly baked naan wafting through the air. But within the dimly lit chamber of Aryan's estate, an invisible dagger had been thrust into his back.

It was Yusuf who had brought him the news first. The old ascetic had arrived unannounced, his eyes heavy with an unspoken sorrow.

"Aryan," Yusuf had said, his voice a whisper against the roaring fire in the room. "You trust too easily."

Aryan had frowned. "What do you mean?"

And then the truth had unfolded before him like a cruel tapestry.

Faizan—the man Aryan had once called his brother, the one he had trusted above all others, despite not sharing the same blood—had shattered that trust with a single act of betrayal. For nothing more than a pouch of gold, Faizan had sold the trade secrets of Aryan's growing empire to a rival merchant, undoing years of unwavering loyalty, shared struggles, and sacred oaths. The man who had once sworn to stand beside him, through triumph and turmoil alike, had instead become the silent architect of his downfall.

At first, Aryan refused to believe it. He stormed through the halls of his estate, his heart a battlefield between denial and fury. Had they not broken bread together? Had they not spent long nights dreaming of the future, making promises of loyalty beneath the starlit sky?

But when Aryan confronted Faizan, there was no denial.

Faizan had stood there, expressionless, as if the weight of betrayal had already been accepted. "I did what I had to," he had said, his voice lacking remorse. "We all do, Aryan. In the end, everyone serves their own survival."

Aryan had felt something inside him shatter. It wasn't just the betrayal—it was the way Faizan had spoken, as though loyalty was merely a currency to be spent and discarded. The man Aryan had trusted above all others had looked at him not as a friend but as an opportunity lost.

The rage that followed was unlike anything he had ever known. It clawed at his chest, demanded blood for blood, a wound for a wound. He wanted Faizan to suffer, to know the weight of his own actions. Revenge seemed like the only road forward.

And so, Aryan had made his choice.

Faizan was cast out. His name was erased from the ledgers, his presence removed from Aryan's world as though he had never existed. But even as the act of vengeance was complete, Aryan felt no victory.

Days turned to weeks, and though his empire continued to grow, an emptiness lingered. The betrayal had changed something within him. The laughter of old friends now felt distant, the warmth of companionship something he no longer trusted.

Yusuf had seen it in his eyes.

"Revenge is an easy road," Yusuf had said one evening, as they stood overlooking the vast empire Aryan had built. "But tell me, Aryan, has it healed you?"

Aryan had no answer. Because even as power rested at his feet, he realised the truth—revenge had not undone the betrayal. It had only deepened the wound.

And now, as he stood in his grand estate, surrounded by wealth but devoid of true companionship, Aryan finally asked himself:

Had Faizan truly taken something from him that night? Or had the betrayal simply revealed what he had always feared—that trust, once broken, was something that could never be restored?

For the first time, Aryan wondered if justice was ever about punishment—or if it was about finding the strength to let go of the past.

That night, he sought out his old mentor, the ascetic Yusuf, who sat beneath a dimly lit archway, sipping tea. His eyes held the wisdom of countless storms, unmoved by the tempests of men.

Aryan poured out his heart. "Tell me, Yusuf, is justice about punishment or understanding?"

Yusuf set his cup down gently. "Justice," he said, "is not a sword. It is a mirror. A man who seeks justice must first see himself clearly. If you hold anger in your heart, you will call revenge by the name of justice."

Aryan frowned. "But how can one move on when betrayal wounds so deeply?"

Yusuf gestured toward the vast night sky. "Do you see that star? It was born from fire, yet it does not burn. It gives light instead. Pain is fire, my son—you can let it consume you, or you can let it illuminate your path."

The words struck Aryan. He had been feeding the fire, believing revenge would bring closure. Instead, it had only deepened the emptiness within.

"Then is forgiveness a greater act of power than retaliation?" Aryan asked.

Yusuf smiled. "Forgiveness is not weakness. It is the strength to walk forward when the world begs you to turn back."

That night, Aryan's heart grew heavy with realisation. Revenge had chained him to the past, while justice—true justice—demanded he rise beyond his pain.

CHAPTER XVI

The Paradox of Laws

"Not all prisons have walls. Some are built from unspoken regrets, some from the fear of change, and the worst of all—from the lies we tell ourselves to avoid the truth."

— Shree Shambav

The Burden of Justice

The courtroom was heavy with the weight of unspoken emotions. The flickering torches along the stone walls cast long shadows, as if the very room itself mourned the fate of the accused. Before Aryan stood a frail man, his clothes tattered, his hands calloused from years of struggle. His crime? Stealing a loaf of bread to feed his starving child.

The judge's gavel struck the polished wood, a sound that echoed like a sentence already passed. "The law is clear," the judge intoned. "Theft, no matter the intent, demands punishment."

Aryan remained silent, yet his mind drifted to another time—another betrayal, another courtroom of sorts.

A Court Without Walls

Years ago, Aryan had stood before Rahim, his mentor, accused of a crime of his own—not of theft, but of ambition.

"You made a deal without consulting me," Rahim had said, his voice carrying the disappointment of a father who had expected better. "You risked everything for profit."

Aryan had defended himself. "I only did what was necessary to expand our reach. Was it not for the greater good?"

Rahim sighed. "Do laws protect us, or do they confine us, Aryan? You followed the rules of trade, but at what cost?"

Now, as Aryan looked at the accused man trembling before the court, those words rang in his ears. Laws maintained order, but did they always serve justice?

A Man Against the Law

Aryan stepped forward, his voice calm but firm. "Do laws protect us, or do they confine us?" he asked.

The judge did not look up. "Laws uphold order."

Aryan's eyes scanned the courtroom. Merchants, noblemen, and scholars sat in rigid silence, their wealth insulating them from the desperation of the man on trial. "And when is it just to challenge the rules set before us?" he continued.

The judge sighed. "Order must be preserved. If we make exceptions, chaos will follow."

Aryan shook his head. "A child cries from hunger, and you speak of order? A father breaks a rule to save his son, and you call it chaos?" His voice was sharp now, demanding. "Are we truly free if we live only by rules written by others?"

This time, the judge had no answer.

Aryan turned to the accused. "What would you have done if your child starved?"

The man's voice was barely above a whisper. "I would have stolen again."

The air in the courtroom grew thick. No one spoke.

The Unwritten Law

That night, as Aryan walked the streets of the city, he saw a beggar share his last piece of bread with a stray dog. No law had commanded him to do so. No punishment loomed over him should he refuse. It was then that Aryan understood—morality was not dictated by law. It existed beyond it.

Some laws bound men, while others freed them.

The next morning, Aryan stood before the judge once more, not as a witness, but as an advocate. "Punish him if you must," Aryan said. "But if theft is a crime, then so is a world where a father must steal to keep his child alive."

And for the first time, Aryan understood the weight of true power—not in punishment, but in the wisdom to know when to forgive, when to stand against injustice, and when to let go of the ghosts of vengeance.

CHAPTER XVII

Freedom and Its Hidden Chains

"Nothing truly belongs to us—not people, not wealth, not even time. The tighter we grasp, the more life slips through our fingers. Only in letting go do we finally hold the infinite."

— Shree Shambav

The air in the grand hall was thick with the scent of burning incense. Aryan sat at the far end of the opulent chamber, watching a wealthy merchant, Junaid, pace restlessly. Piles of gold coins gleamed under the soft glow of the oil lamps, yet Junaid's face was lined with worry.

"They will come for it," Junaid muttered, wringing his hands. "The thieves, the betrayers. Even my sons look at my fortune like wolves circling a wounded deer."

Aryan remained silent, staring at the trembling man before him. Junaid had everything—land, wealth, power—but he was a prisoner in his own palace, his nights sleepless, his heart heavy with fear.

That night, Aryan walked through the city streets, his mind drifting to the past. He remembered his youth, when he and Rohan had run barefoot across the fields, when laughter was abundant and worries were scarce. They had dreamed of wealth, believing it would make them free. But what if they had been freer then, in their innocence, than he was now?

His thoughts were interrupted by a burst of laughter. At the corner of a narrow street, a group of beggars huddled around a small fire. Their clothes were tattered, their feet bare, yet they laughed—deep, unburdened laughter that seemed to rise from the very core of their being.

One of them, an old man with silver hair and piercing eyes, looked up and met Aryan's gaze.

"You look lost, traveller," the old man said.

Aryan hesitated before stepping closer. "Perhaps I am."

"What is it you seek?" the man asked.

Aryan thought of his long journey—the countless riches he had amassed, the luxuries he had surrounded himself with—yet, it was not wealth that followed him into his dreams, but the treasures that still eluded him. The map, worn and creased from years of being folded and unfolded, felt like an extension of his own soul—marked with the ink of his desires, etched with the weight of his relentless pursuit. He had carried it for so long, tracing its paths over and over, believing it would lead him to the fortune. But was it truly the treasure he sought, or had the hunt itself become the chain that bound him?

"I seek something valuable," Aryan said at last.

The old man chuckled. "And what if you find it? Will you finally be free?"

Aryan frowned. "Wealth brings freedom."

The beggar shook his head. "Wealth brings choices, but not always freedom. The man with nothing fears nothing. The man with everything fears losing it all."

Aryan was about to argue, but the words struck something deep within him. He had spent years amassing riches, securing his place among the powerful. Yet, had he ever felt truly free?

His mind wandered back to his treasure hunt. He had risked everything for that fabled hoard, believing it would be the key to his ultimate freedom. But as he stood among those who owned nothing yet seemed to possess everything—peace, laughter, simplicity—he wondered:

Was freedom measured by what he owned, or by what no longer owned him?

He turned to the old man once more. "Does power grant liberty, or does it tighten the chains around us?"

The old man smiled. "Tell me, traveller—who is freer? The bird soaring through the sky, or the one kept in a golden cage?"

Aryan exhaled. He had once admired kings, men of power and fortune. But now he saw their hidden chains—paranoia, distrust, loneliness.

The beggar continued, "The freest man is not the one who can do anything, but the one who needs nothing."

Aryan looked down at his hands. How many things had he clung to, believing they would liberate him, only to find himself more burdened?

And then, a final question whispered through his mind, touching the core of his treasure hunt:

If wealth buys comfort but not peace, then what is the true currency of freedom?

For years, he had chased a treasure he believed would complete him. But now, standing in the warmth of a simple fire, surrounded by those who had nothing yet lacked nothing, he realised:

Perhaps the treasure he sought was not gold, but something far rarer—**the ability to let go.**

That night, as Aryan walked away from the fire, the map in his pocket felt heavier than ever.

CHAPTER XVIII

The Battle Between Heart and Mind

"Some roads take us forward, but at the cost of what we leave behind. The question is—was the journey worth the silence of those we once loved?"

– Shree Shambav

One evening, as the setting sun bathed the city in hues of fire and gold, Aryan wandered through the marketplace, lost in thought. The weight of his empire, the echo of his past, and the face of Meera—forever imprinted in his heart—warred within him. His mind whispered of unfinished ambitions, of wealth still to be conquered, while his heart ached for the warmth of love, for the place where his soul had first known peace.

It was then that he saw the old traveller.

Bent with age but bright in his gaze, the man sat by the fountain, watching the passersby. Something about him seemed strangely familiar. Aryan, drawn by an inexplicable force, approached him.

The traveller smiled. "You seem burdened, man. Tell me, what weighs on your soul?"

Aryan hesitated. Could a stranger understand the war raging within him? Yet, in that moment, words poured out like a dam breaking.

"I have built an empire," he said. "I have conquered wealth, lands, and power. But I stand at a crossroads. Should I chase greatness further or return to those I left behind?"

The traveller chuckled. "Do you know the story of the two birds?"

Aryan shook his head.

The old man continued, "Once, two birds were given the choice between two trees. One bore golden fruits, rare and magnificent. The other had simple branches but was home to their loved ones, their nest. One bird chose the golden tree, believing it would bring happiness. The other chose home, believing it would bring warmth. The first bird ate gold but never found peace. The second bird lived in love but wondered if it had abandoned greatness. Both longed for what the other had."

Aryan clenched his fists. "Then what is the answer? Which bird was right?"

The traveller smiled. "Neither was wrong, but neither was entirely right. The wisest path is not choosing one tree over the other—it is finding a way to carry the fruit of one back to the nest of the other."

Aryan stood frozen. It was as if the very question tormenting him had been answered in a single stroke of wisdom.

That night, as he sat in his grand hall, staring at the map of treasure he had carried all these years, he understood: *The greatest treasure was never gold or power. It was knowing how to bridge the dreams of the mind with the longing of the heart.*

CHAPTER XIX

The Gift Hidden in Pain

"We are taught to chase our dreams, but what are we left with when those dreams demand the abandonment of the ones we love?"

— Shree Shambav

The night was silent, save for the crackling fire before Aryan. He sat by the riverbank, watching the reflection of the flames flicker upon the dark water. Across from him sat Yuvan, an old wanderer with eyes that had seen more pain than most.

Aryan exhaled deeply, the weight of his past pressing against his chest. "I used to think pain was a curse," he admitted. "That suffering was life's cruelty, stripping me of everything I loved."

Yuvan poked the fire with his staff, sending sparks into the night sky. "Is pain a curse," he asked, "or is it a hidden teacher guiding us to strength?"

Aryan's jaw clenched, and his fists tightened as he stared into the crackling fire, the shadows dancing across his face. "Pain never felt like a teacher," he said, his voice rough, burdened by the weight of years lost. "When I left my parents behind in the village, all I could feel was emptiness—the loss of home, the absence of their love. When Faizan betrayed me, it was like a knife being twisted in my gut, shattering everything I'd once trusted. And when I left Meera, the one person who truly understood me, in pursuit of a treasure I thought would fill the void—regret consumed me like a slow, burning flame that never went out. But when I lost Rahim—my mentor, my father in so many ways—what did pain teach me, Yuvan? What wisdom did it offer except how to lose everything that ever truly mattered?"

Yuvan smiled faintly. "Did it not also teach you resilience? Did it not carve wisdom into your soul? Tell me, Aryan, does suffering break us, or does it carve us into something greater?"

Aryan was silent. He thought he had spent in sorrow, and yet, he had survived. He had risen. The wounds had shaped him, just as a sculptor's chisel shapes raw stone into art.

"But why must it be this way?" Aryan asked bitterly. "Why does happiness feel so fleeting, and pain so permanent?"

Yuvan reached for a small clay cup, filled it with water from the river, and placed it in Aryan's hands. "Drink."

Aryan sipped. The water was cold, refreshing.

"Now imagine if you had never known thirst," Yuvan said. "Would you truly appreciate this drink?"

Aryan's fingers tightened around the cup. He understood. *Can we truly appreciate joy without having known deep sorrow?*

For the first time, he saw the truth. The nights of despair had given depth to the moments of light. Without sorrow, joy would be shallow—like an ocean without depth, a song without silence.

Yuvan gazed into the fire. "Many spend their lives running from pain. They numb it, drown it, curse it. But tell me, Aryan, is healing found in escaping pain or in embracing and understanding it?"

Aryan closed his eyes. He had spent years chasing power, wealth, and distractions, thinking they would erase his wounds. But now, sitting here, he realised: running had never healed him. Facing it had.

He looked up at Yuvan, a quiet understanding settling over him. "Pain did not destroy me," he murmured. "It shaped me."

And with that, Aryan finally saw pain not as his enemy but as the fire that had forged him.

PART FIVE

Finding What Was Never Lost

We often search for what was never lost, only hidden in the corners of our hearts, waiting to be remembered."

-Shree Shambav

CHAPTER XX

The Fragility of Friendship

"True friendship is not measured by what you can give, but by what you've given when you had nothing to offer."

— Shree Shambav

Aryan sat alone in the grand hall, his fingers tracing the intricate carvings on the armrest of his chair. The weight of the silence pressed heavily on him. Outside, the evening sun cast long shadows over the opulent mansion, but within, there was an emptiness that no wealth could fill. His thoughts drifted back to the days when he had nothing but the companionship of his friends had been everything.

He thought of Rohan, his childhood friend, the one who had always been there by his side. Rohan was a few years older, but their bond had been unbreakable. They had run through the fields together, shared dreams and fears, and laughed under the shade of the old banyan tree in their village. Aryan remembered the way Rohan's eyes had always sparkled with sincerity, how he never asked for anything in return for his kindness.

And then there was Suraj, the elder friend who had always offered wisdom when Aryan needed it most. Suraj had never expected anything from him. His loyalty wasn't measured by what Aryan could give but by what they shared in their hearts. "Success can change a man, Aryan," Suraj once said. "But the true test is whether your soul remains the same, whether you remain the same for those who were with you when you had nothing."

Aryan chuckled softly, his eyes closing as memories flooded back. He missed those simple days when the future was uncertain but his friends were constant. But now, surrounded by riches, he had few friends, and fewer still who didn't come with strings attached.

His thoughts turned to the people he had met on his journey—the ones who had left indelible marks on his soul. Rahim, the godfather figure who had taken him in when he was nothing but a young trader desperate to learn. Rahim's wisdom had shaped Aryan into the man he was today, but now, amid his power, he wondered if he could ever repay the debt of gratitude he owed him. Peter, the merchant from Taxila, had shared his struggles and stories of old when Aryan was just starting in his trading career. Peter had never sought wealth or status; he had simply shared his heart.

Joseph, the innocent boy whose curiosity and purity had opened Aryan's hearts to a different kind of world, one where love and kindness were more valuable than gold. Omar, the wise advisor who had always been honest with Aryan, even when the truth was harsh. And Yusuf, his old mentor, whose teachings about restraint and wisdom still guided Aryan to this day.

Baba Govind's voice echoed in his mind, the man who had warned him against the very journey he now embarked upon. His words, "To leave the known behind is not the hardest part, my boy. It is to walk forward when doubt grips you, when the weight of the past calls you back. The road ahead will not just test your feet—it will test your soul."

Aryan's jaw tightened as he reflected on those words. His wealth and power had isolated him. The people around him—those who now vied for his attention—were not the same as the ones who had stood by him when he had nothing. They wanted something from him. They wanted his favour, his influence. Aryan could see the difference between those who genuinely cared and those who simply sought to use him for their gain.

The Questions Hung Heavily in His Heart:

Does power isolate, or does it reveal who our true friends are?

He remembered the laughter shared with his old friends—Rohan, Suraj, and the others. The pure joy in those moments had been simple, untarnished by the weight of expectation. The people in his life now, in the opulence of his wealth, seemed so different. Was it that power had isolated him, or had it merely revealed who had been there for the right reasons and who was only drawn to his status?

Can a friendship withstand the changes success brings?

He thought of how easily people had come and gone in his life since he'd attained success. Those who had once walked with him in humble circumstances now stayed at a distance, and new faces were drawn to him by the magnetism of his power. But had those friendships, once forged in the simplicity of shared struggles, been altered by the success he had achieved? He wasn't sure. And that uncertainty gnawed at him.

Is loneliness a consequence of ambition or a self-imposed exile?

At night, when he lay alone in his vast, empty bed, loneliness crept in like a silent visitor. He had everything a man could desire: riches, power, respect—but no true companionship. Was this loneliness a natural result of the ambition he had chased for so long, or had he, in his pursuit of dreams, built a self-imposed prison around himself? The thought lingered in his mind, but the answer remained elusive.

How do we discern between true friends and those drawn only to our status?

Aryan had been deceived before, tricked by those who seemed genuine but were only after his fortune. How could he know who truly cared for him as a person and who merely wanted to bask in the light of his success? In his heart, he longed for the simple friendships he had once had, but how could he find that again in a world where everything seemed to have a price?

As the questions swirled in his mind, he realised that the friendships he cherished from his past were like rare gems—precious and few. And the more he sought power, the more he realised that true companionship was a treasure far more valuable than anything money could buy.

The Answer Came Slowly, like a Whisper in the Wind:

True friends are the ones who remain with you when the world shifts beneath your feet, when wealth and power no longer matter. They are the ones who stood by you before you had anything, and they will stand by you when you have nothing left. The others—the ones drawn to your status—will fade away when the spotlight dims.

Aryan stood up and walked toward the window, looking out at the city he had built, the empire he had crafted with his own hands. The golden lights twinkled like stars in the distance, but they felt cold, distant. His heart yearned for the warmth of true friendship, for the laughter and honesty he once shared with those who had known him before the world knew his name.

He closed his eyes, a soft smile playing on his lips as he remembered Rohan's words: *"True friends are the ones who help you carry the weight of your dreams, not those who simply want to ride on them."*

The night felt quiet, almost peaceful, as Aryan sat back down in his chair. The power he had amassed felt less important now. He realised that in the end, the treasure he had been seeking all along was not gold or riches but the bonds of genuine friendship.

CHAPTER XXI

The Power of Silent Prayers

———·····━━━◇━━━·····———

"Sometimes the prayers we whisper into the silence are the ones that shape us the most."

Shree Shambav

The moon hung heavy in the sky, casting an ethereal glow on the worn stone steps that led to the ancient temple at the outskirts of Aryan's mansion. The air was cool, thick with the weight of his unspoken thoughts. Aryan, once a man driven by the fire of ambition, now found himself kneeling on the cold stone floor, the weight of his journey pressing down on him like a thousand boulders.

The temple was silent, save for the soft whispers of the wind through the trees and the occasional flutter of wings from a distant bird. Aryan closed his eyes, his heart racing, not from fear, but from the deep ache that had begun to gnaw at him over the years. He had built empires, amassed wealth, and seen things that few could even dream of. But now, as he knelt there, he felt something profound—something that had eluded him for all these years.

The prayers he had once uttered in hopes of gaining power, wealth, and success seemed hollow now. They had been answered, but they had led him to an emptiness he could never have imagined. He prayed for something different now. Not riches, not glory, but peace. Peace that could only come from a return to what he had lost long ago—his home, his family, and the simple joys that had once made his heart sing.

"Will they still remember me?" Aryan whispered to the empty air, his voice barely a breath. "Will the village recognise the man I've become, or will they see only the boy who left, the one who dreamed of treasures in lands far away? I have crossed seas, climbed mountains, and battled every storm to find this fortune... but what good is it if I cannot find my way home?"

His tears fell silently onto the stone beneath him. His heart felt heavy, burdened by a longing he could not explain. The years of chasing treasures, of amassing gold and jewels, had made him a man of wealth, but not a man of peace. The treasures he sought—whatever they were—had not brought him the sense of completion he so desperately needed. They had instead driven him further from what truly mattered.

"When will I see the people who really cared for me?" he thought, his mind wandering to his parents, to Rohan, Suraj, and Meera—those whose names were etched into the very core of his soul. *"Who will help me find my place again? What is the treasure that haunts me so? What could it possibly be, if not the peace I have longed for all these years?"*

Aryan stood, his knees sore from kneeling, but his heart strangely lighter. He had come seeking answers, but in the silence of the temple, in the stillness of his own soul, he began to realise something. The treasure he had been searching for all along had never been a chest filled with gold. It had always been the peace that could only come from returning to his roots, from reconnecting with the ones he loved, and most importantly, from coming back to himself.

As the wind rustled the ancient trees around him, Aryan asked the questions that had plagued him for so long:

"Do prayers change our fate, or do they change us?" he asked aloud, his voice trembling with the weight of the years that had passed. He had prayed for success, but had it not been his own ambition that had shaped his fate all along? Could his prayers have guided him to a place of peace if he had asked for it sooner?

"Why do some prayers go unanswered?" Aryan continued, his voice tinged with confusion. "I've asked for so much, but have I asked for the right things? Why, after everything I've gained, do I feel so empty? Is this what fate had in store for me all along, or is there something I missed?"

The wind seemed to pause, as though waiting for his next words, before he murmured, **"Is faith stronger than fate?"** He thought of all the people who had told him that fate was something beyond his control, that the course of his life was predestined. But Aryan had always fought against it—he had chosen his own path, battled his own demons. Now, he wondered if faith, the belief in something greater than himself, could be the key to breaking the chains that bound him.

Finally, he whispered, **"Do we pray for guidance, or for outcomes we desire?"** He had prayed for wealth and success, but in truth, he had never prayed for the wisdom to understand what he truly needed. Did he pray for the answers that would bring him closer to his heart, or had he only sought to feed his ego, his insatiable desire for more?

The silence of the night settled around him, deep and thick, like a blanket wrapping him in its stillness. And in that silence, Aryan realised something profound: his journey was never about the treasure, the riches, or the fame. It was about the questions, the quiet reflections, and the slow return to what had always been within him—peace, love, and the sense of belonging.

As he stood and turned to leave the temple, Aryan finally understood: it was not fate that had brought him to this place, but the prayers he had whispered in the stillness of his heart, unanswered, perhaps, but always shaping him. The treasure was never far from his grasp—it had always been there, waiting for him to recognise it.

And as the first light of dawn touched the horizon, Aryan knew that his journey had not yet ended. It had merely shifted.

CHAPTER XXII

The Journey from Pleasure to Purpose

"Pleasure is like water cupped in the hands—refreshing for a moment, but it always slips through the fingers. Purpose, however, is the river that never runs dry."

— Shree Shambav

Aryan stood at the edge of a rugged coastline, the wind lashing against his skin, carrying the scent of salt and distant memories. The sea stretched endlessly before him, its waves crashing with a restless hunger—much like his own. He had travelled far, crossed mountains and deserts, gained wealth and power, yet here he was, standing next to an old friend who had never left Taxila, wondering if he had been chasing shadows all along.

Peter, his companion, stood beside him. The years had weathered him, but there was a stillness in his eyes, a quiet wisdom Aryan had once overlooked. Peter had not sought riches, nor had he wandered in search of distant lands. He had chosen a different path—a simple one, yet full of meaning.

Peter gazed at the horizon, his voice almost lost to the wind. "I remember the first time I set foot on these shores. I was young, hungry for adventure, thinking the world would hand me fortune, fame, and pleasure."

Aryan clenched his fists, staring at the endless waters. "And did it?" he asked, his voice thick with the weight of his disillusionment.

Peter turned to him, a half-smile on his lips. "No. But it gave me something far greater—the understanding that true joy doesn't come from what we take, but from what we give. Land, people, lessons… they are not treasures to possess, Aryan. They are stories to live."

Aryan exhaled, the tightness in his chest growing. "I thought power, wealth… these things would make me whole. But even with all that, I feel more lost than ever."

Peter placed a hand on his shoulder. "It's easy to mistake pleasure for purpose. Comfort may bring ease, but it never fulfils the soul. Pleasure is fleeting, Aryan—like the waves against these rocks. It comes and goes. But purpose… purpose is like the river. It may bend, slow, even disappear underground, but it never ceases."

A deep chuckle interrupted their thoughts. They turned to see a man approaching—tall, with sun-kissed skin and piercing eyes that had seen more of the world than either of them. Captain Alistair, the Scottish explorer, who had charted lands unknown, crossed deserts few dared, and sailed waters that swallowed entire fleets. His presence alone carried the weight of untold stories.

Alistair greeted them with a knowing grin. "Aye, lads, ye look like ye've walked too many roads and still can't find home. Let me tell ye something—the treasure ye seek ain't buried in gold or locked away in vaults. It's in the meaning ye give to the life ye live."

Aryan's gaze sharpened. "I thought treasure was something tangible. Something waiting to be found."

The Captain laughed, a sound rich with experience. "I've sailed the seven seas, crossed deserts that stretch longer than a man's lifetime, and I tell ye, the wealthiest men weren't those with gold, but those who gave their lives meaning. Helping others, leaving legacies, sharing their wisdom—that is wealth, lad. That is what endures."

Peter nodded. "It's not about what you achieve, Aryan. It's about what you give meaning to. Comfort fades, but purpose lasts. The work you do, the lives you touch—that's what makes a journey worthwhile."

Aryan swallowed, his mind a storm of memories—Meera, his parents, Faizan's betrayal. "But how do I find it? Purpose, I mean. I've spent my life chasing pleasure, power. How do I know if what I do now will bring fulfilment?"

Alistair's gaze softened. "Ye don't find purpose, lad. It finds ye, in the choices ye make, in the lives ye change. Purpose ain't in the riches ye hoard, but in the love ye give, the kindness ye show. It's not waiting for ye at the end of a journey—it's in every step ye take."

As the sun dipped beyond the horizon, Aryan felt something shift within him. The treasure he had sought was never about gold or land—it was about meaning. And for the first time, he saw a different path ahead.

That night, as they rested on the island, Aryan decided to show them the map he had carried for years. The map that haunted his dreams, the one that had led him down this endless path.

Before dawn, Aryan woke and wandered the shore. Looking at the vast ocean before him, he whispered a silent prayer. If there was any hope left of finding the treasure, it rested with Alistair. "Let him be the last hope…" he murmured. "I've searched every network, consulted the most powerful men, but none have heard of the place I seek—the golden desert, hidden behind mountains, across an ocean."

For years, the same dream had haunted him—golden sands stretching into infinity, an ancient chest buried beneath a lone tree, the wind whispering his name. He had crossed lands, forged alliances, lost love, and gained power. But the treasure still eluded him.

After breakfast, Aryan turned to Alistair. "Captain, I need your help. I have searched for this place for years. It has been in my dreams since childhood."

Alistair's eyes narrowed with curiosity. "Ye left behind home, love, and kin… for a dream?"

Aryan nodded. "Yes. I cannot return home without finding it."

Peter interjected, "Captain, I have known Aryan since we were boys. He will stop at nothing to achieve his dreams. We both started as simple traders, but his mind… his relentless curiosity, his talent for strategy, his way with people—it has taken him across borders, to power and fame. People listen when he speaks. They trust his judgment."

Alistair held out his hand. "Show me."

Aryan unrolled the worn, tattered map. The edges were frayed, the ink faded. He had scribbled notes, traced lines over and over, trying to make sense of the visions that had led him here.

Alistair studied it carefully, tracing his fingers over the markings. "According to this, ye need to cross an ocean, climb a treacherous hill, and walk a desert of golden sand, where a lone tree stands."

The Captain closed his eyes, deep in thought. Minutes passed in silence. Then, he exhaled. "Give me some days. I keep records of every place I travel, mapping them as I go. This place… it feels familiar. But I need to check my diaries."

Aryan felt a spark of hope ignite within him. After years of chasing ghosts, after endless dead ends, here was a man who had perhaps seen what no one else had.

For the first time in years, Aryan dared to believe. Perhaps he was finally one step closer to the treasure that had defined his life's journey.

PART SIX

The Final Treasure

We often search for what was never lost, only hidden in the corners of our hearts, waiting to be remembered."

-Shree Shambav

CHAPTER XXIII

The Journey's End

"True friendship is not measured by what you can give, but by what you've given when you had nothing to offer."

— Shree Shambav

The Price of Time and the Weight of Destiny

The grand hall of Aryan's palatial home was dimly lit, the flickering glow of the lanterns casting long shadows against the stone walls. It had been months since their last meeting, and now, Peter and Captain Alistair sat before him, their faces etched with untold burdens.

Aryan welcomed them warmly, his voice carrying both affection and curiosity. "It was a great meeting on that island," he said, pouring wine into their goblets, "a revelation, indeed." His eyes lingered on Alistair, sensing the weight in the old sailor's gaze. "But something tells me you have come for a reason."

Alistair hesitated, his fingers tightening around the wooden goblet. Aryan noticed the slight tremble in his hands. His heartbeat quickened—was this the moment he had long awaited? Had Alistair finally discovered the place in his dreams, the treasure hidden beneath golden sands?

"Immediately, please," Aryan urged, leaning forward.

Peter placed a firm hand on Aryan's shoulder. "Captain is asking a favour from you," he interjected gently.

Aryan frowned. "A favour? From me?"

The Captain lifted his weary eyes, tears brimming at their edges. He exhaled heavily, his chest rising and falling as though the weight of years had suddenly grown unbearable.

"I was a sailor once," he began, his voice barely above a whisper. "I fell in love with a woman on an island I had travelled to—her name was Alba. The moment I saw her, it was as if the gods themselves had woven her into my destiny. We were married within months."

Aryan listened, his anticipation shifting into a quiet, solemn stillness.

"One day, I set sail on a routine journey," Alistair continued, his voice cracking. "But fate had other plans. A cruel storm ravaged the seas, tossing my ship into oblivion. I watched my crew—my brothers—disappear into the abyss one by one. Seven men drowned that night. I alone survived, stranded on an island I had never seen before."

Peter's gaze lowered, knowing the pain of loss all too well.

"The island was dense, its terrain unforgiving. I wandered aimlessly, my body battered and my heart heavier than my limbs. When I finally reached a village, the people there—kind souls—nursed me back to life. Two men, Mateo and Henry, took me in, their families fed me, clothed me, and for years, they became my only solace. But the memory of Alba tormented me. Did she think I had abandoned her? Did she mourn me as dead?"

Alistair's fingers trembled as he clenched them into a fist. "Every night, I dreamed of her. I had nothing—no ship, no money, no means to return. But Mateo's grandchild, Lucas, became my light in that darkness. His innocent laughter, his questions, his companionship—they kept me from losing myself completely."

Aryan listened in silence, the weight of Alistair's sorrow settling over the room like a thick mist.

"Years passed. I learned the ways of the land, trading herbs to nearby islands. Slowly, I gathered enough wealth to build a boat. And when I finally returned to Alba's island…"

He closed his eyes, a deep breath shuddering through his body.

"There was nothing left."

Aryan swallowed hard.

"A tsunami had devastated the island. The people were gone. Alba… was gone."

A long silence filled the hall, the only sound the distant crackling of the hearth.

Peter ran a hand over his face, whispering a prayer under his breath.

Alistair's voice was hoarse when he spoke again. "I buried my past in the tides and continued my trade. Wealth came easily, but loneliness stayed. I built ships, hired men, and gave the people of Electra island opportunities, but in my heart, I remained a man lost at sea."

He looked directly at Aryan now, his eyes filled with desperation.

"Then, one day, Mateo's smile faded. His grandson, Lucas—the boy who once saved me from despair—was dying. A rare disease is claiming his life, and the only cure lies on Crystal Island. But the island is ruled by a powerful Sultan, and no one without his favour can step foot there."

A single tear escaped the Captain's eye. "Aryan, I need your help. Your influence, your power—perhaps it can save a young life."

Without hesitation, Aryan nodded. "Consider it done."

Peter exhaled a breath of relief, gripping Alistair's shoulder in reassurance.

"Stay with me," Aryan said. "We will prepare for the journey."

That night, as Aryan stood on his terrace, staring up at the stars, he felt a strange sense of irony settle over him. He had believed Alistair had come with a solution for his treasure hunt, but destiny had shifted its course.

"Divine," Aryan whispered, his gaze never leaving the stars, "you must have a reason."

CHAPTER XXIV

The Island of Echoes

"The ocean does not break a sailor; it reveals him. It strips him of all but his will to return home."

— Shree Shambav

As the first rays of dawn painted the sky in soft gold, Aryan wandered through the village, his feet treading paths that felt both foreign and familiar. The air was thick with the scent of earth and crushed herbs, the distant hum of the ocean whispering against the cliffs.

He passed small, thatched huts nestled between towering trees. Vines curled around wooden fences, and the morning breeze carried the distant sound of children's laughter. The village was alive, yet something about it felt like an echo from his past, as if his soul had once belonged here.

Davina, the young woman who had welcomed them the night before, was kneeling near a stone mortar, grinding herbs into fine powder. As she saw Aryan, she offered a gentle smile.

"You're up early," she said, brushing loose strands of hair from her face.

"I couldn't sleep," Aryan admitted. He looked around, his eyes scanning the landscape. "This place… I don't know why, but it feels like I've been here before."

Davina's smile faded slightly. "Perhaps your heart remembers what your mind has forgotten," she said, her voice carrying a quiet wisdom.

Before Aryan could respond, Captain Alistair and Peter approached. Peter carried a loaf of freshly baked bread in his hands, its warmth still visible in the steam that curled from it.

"Good morning, lad," Captain Alistair greeted, his sharp eyes observing Aryan's pensive mood. "Ye seem troubled."

Aryan shook his head, forcing a smile. "Just lost in thought."

Peter handed Aryan a piece of bread. "The villagers bake this with a mix of special herbs. It's meant to bring strength."

Aryan took a bite, the flavour earthy yet comforting. It was unlike anything he had ever tasted, yet oddly familiar.

Davina's father, an elderly man with deep lines carved into his face like a map of time, emerged from a nearby hut. His hands, roughened by years of tending to herbs, trembled slightly as he carried a wooden staff.

"You seek the Burdock Root," the old man said, his voice rasping like dry leaves.

Aryan turned to him with a nod. "Yes. A young boy's life depends on it."

The old man's gaze sharpened, studying Aryan intently. "The root does not simply grow where one looks. It chooses who finds it."

Captain Alistair scoffed lightly. "Lad, it's a plant, not a treasure chest."

But Aryan wasn't so sure. He had seen too many coincidences in his life, too many paths aligning as if fate itself was guiding him.

Davina stepped forward. "The Burdock Root grows on the neighbouring island, but the journey is not easy. The currents are dangerous, and the land is guarded by those who believe outsiders have no right to take from it."

Peter frowned. "Then how do we get it?"

Davina looked at Aryan. "Perhaps the island will only allow those with the right intentions to enter."

Aryan held her gaze. In her deep brown eyes, he saw something—an unspoken understanding, a familiarity that sent a strange ache through his chest.

He exhaled, looking toward the horizon. The sea stretched before them, an uncharted path leading to something far greater than just an herb.

"Then we leave at dawn," Aryan said. "If destiny has brought us here, we must see where it leads."

The old man nodded solemnly. "Then be prepared, Aryan. Sometimes, in seeking to save another's life, you may end up finding your own."

The Journey of Fate

The village was slowly coming to life as the sun climbed higher, casting golden hues across the dense forest that surrounded it. Birds chirped in the distance, their melodies blending with the faint rustling of the morning breeze.

Aryan, Peter, and Captain Alistair sat near the stone hearth of Davina's modest home, the smell of freshly brewed herbal tea filling the air. The morning had been peaceful until Davina spoke, her voice trembling as she recounted her child's suffering.

"My son… his breathing grows weaker by the day," she said, her hands clutching the hem of her dress as if holding onto the last thread of hope. "My father has tried everything, but we cannot find the right herbs. We have searched every island we could reach, yet nothing…" Her voice broke, and silent tears rolled down her cheeks.

Aryan, who had seen fortunes built and empires rise, felt an unfamiliar heaviness settle in his chest. He had always believed in power, in wealth, in the pursuit of greatness—but here was a mother, breaking under the weight of helplessness.

"Why must the heavens test those who love the most?" he murmured, almost to himself.

Captain Alistair leaned forward, his expression unreadable. "What is the disease, Davina?"

She hesitated before whispering, "A rare respiratory ailment. We need Licorice Root, Pippali, Oregano… but we have found none."

A slow smile spread across Captain Alistair's face, his eyes gleaming with an unspoken secret.

Aryan and Peter exchanged puzzled glances. "Why are you smiling?" Peter asked.

Without answering, the Captain reached for his leather satchel, carefully unfastening its brass buckle. The old, worn bag creaked as he reached inside and pulled out several small cloth pouches. He placed them on the wooden table, his calloused fingers smoothing the fabric before he untied them.

The moment the dried herbs spilled onto the table, Davina gasped, her eyes widening in disbelief.

"This... this is Licorice Root!" she exclaimed, her hands trembling as she picked up the herb. "And Pippali... and Oregano..." Her voice cracked, and tears streamed down her face.

Her father, an elderly man with eyes clouded by time, stepped forward, his gnarled hands touching the herbs with reverence. "Where did you find these?" he asked, his voice barely a whisper.

Captain Alistair smiled gently. "A lifetime at sea has its perks. A sailor must always be prepared. I kept these for emergencies, but fate seems to have led me here for another reason."

Davina dropped to her knees, clutching the herbs to her chest. "You have saved my son," she sobbed.

Peter wiped his own eyes, moved by the moment. Even Aryan, a man hardened by the world, felt something shift within him.

That night, as Davina's father prepared the medicine, the village gathered outside their home, murmuring prayers and lighting lanterns that swayed in the night breeze.

A New Quest

Over the next few days, Aryan, Peter, and Captain Alistair resumed their search for the Burdock Root—the very reason they had come to the island.

One evening, as they sat by the fire, Davina approached them, her gaze filled with curiosity.

"You are not ordinary traders," she observed. "You are wealthy, influential… yet you have come to a remote island, risking your lives for a single herb."

Captain Alistair chuckled, leaning back against the wooden pillar of the porch. "Aye, you're not wrong, lass. But sometimes, the greatest journeys are not for gold or power, but for something far more valuable."

Davina tilted her head. "And what is that?"

Aryan, who had been silent, finally spoke. "A debt repaid. A promise honoured. A life saved." His voice was distant, as if he were speaking not just of the boy they sought to save, but of something buried deep in his own soul.

Davina studied him for a long moment before she nodded. "If it is the Burdock Root you seek, you may find it on the neighbouring island," she said. "But the journey is not easy. The waters are rough, and the island is heavily guarded by those who believe it belongs only to them."

Peter exhaled sharply. "So, we need to be careful."

Davina's gaze flickered with something unreadable. "You will need more than caution. You will need courage."

The next morning, before the first light of dawn touched the ocean's surface, Aryan, Peter, Captain Alistair, and Davina set sail. The journey ahead was uncertain, but one thing was clear—this was no longer just about an herb.

It was about destiny.

CHAPTER XXV

Whispers of Destiny

"A simple act of kindness is like a seed carried by the wind. It may take root in places unseen, growing into something far greater than the one who planted it could ever imagine."

— Shree Shambav

After hours of battling the turbulent waters, they finally reached the island. The docks were lined with well-armed guards, their expressions unreadable under the golden glow of the setting sun. Aryan, Captain Alistair, Peter, and Davina disembarked, their tired feet pressing into the soft earth. The island was unlike anything they had seen before—lush, wealthy, and brimming with life. Unlike the struggling villages they had encountered on their journey, this place thrived with opulence. The streets were paved, the houses grand, and the people well-dressed.

The guards ordered them to wait while they sought permission from the island's owner. As minutes stretched into hours, exhaustion weighed upon them. Finally, as the last light of the sun painted the sky in hues of orange and violet, they were escorted to an enormous estate at the heart of the island.

A grand hall awaited them, dimly lit by flickering torches. Aryan, weary from travel, lowered his head, his body sinking into the comfort of the seat provided. Silence stretched in the vast hall until the doors swung open, revealing a tall, broad-shouldered man with a powerful presence. His smile was warm, yet his gaze held the weight of someone who had seen much in life.

"Welcome, travellers," he said in a voice that resonated through the hall. "Be my guests tonight. We shall discuss your purpose in the morning. You are weary, and this island is not one to host tired souls without first offering them rest."

A grand feast was laid before them, the table adorned with delicacies from across the seas. As Aryan ate, he felt something he hadn't in years—a sense of peace. It was strange, unfamiliar, and yet comforting. He pondered the reason for this feeling, questioning whether it stemmed from the kindness he was showing to the young boy in need of healing. His mind drifted back to a conversation he once had with a child named Joseph—a street boy with innocent eyes who had once asked him, "What is more valuable—gold or kindness?"

Later that night, Aryan stood beneath the vast sky, gazing at the stars that shimmered like scattered diamonds. The cool island breeze wrapped around him, fireflies dancing in the air like tiny lanterns of the night. Memories of his childhood flooded his mind—days when there was no burden of power, no fear of betrayal, no hunger for more. Just the simplicity of existing in a world that had not yet demanded anything from him. For the first time in years, he felt unchained, as if the weight he had carried for so long had momentarily lifted.

Unable to resist the serenity, he lay down on the wooden deck and fell asleep beneath the sky's watchful eyes.

As the first rays of dawn kissed the island, Aryan woke before the others. He wandered through the village, inhaling the crisp morning air, his ears delighting in the songs of hummingbirds. The beauty of the island was unlike anything he had known— a paradise untouched by greed, where life thrived in balance. "This place is heaven," he whispered to himself.

As the sun ascended, Joseph entered the common hall, his presence commanding yet welcoming. "What brings you to my island?" he asked, his eyes scanning the group.

Captain Alistair stepped forward. "Sir, we seek an herb— Burdock Root. A young life depends on it."

Joseph nodded thoughtfully. "We should be able to find it. My men will assist you."

Just then, Aryan entered the hall. The moment Joseph laid eyes on him, his expression changed. His composed demeanour broke, his eyes widening in shock and then glistening with emotion.

"You…" Joseph whispered, his voice trembling. "You are here…"

Aryan looked at him, puzzled.

Joseph took a step forward, tears welling in his eyes. "Street boy… your favourite street boy…"

A sudden realisation struck Aryan like a lightning bolt. His breath hitched, and his eyes widened in disbelief.

Joseph continued, his voice thick with emotion, "I have searched for you for years. Destiny has finally allowed us to meet again."

Peter, Captain Alistair, and Davina exchanged bewildered glances. How could a man of such wealth and power refer to himself as a street boy?

Aryan, unable to contain his emotions, embraced Joseph. The weight of years collapsed in that single moment, as if time had folded upon itself. "My boy... my dear boy... I am happy to see you."

Joseph smiled through his tears. "You are a kind man, Aryan. A compassionate man. A man who can conquer empires, but more importantly, a man who can create destinies for others. I am one of those destinies. There are many others who have flourished because of your guidance. They have longed to see you again."

The conversation continued, nostalgia and emotions filling the air. After an hour, Joseph gave the order, and his men set out in search of the rare herb.

After an intense search, they finally found it—the precious Burdock Root, the key to saving a young boy's life.

As Aryan held the herb in his hands, he felt a strange sense of completion, as if fate had orchestrated every twist and turn of his journey to lead him to this very moment. Perhaps, just perhaps, life was not about seeking riches but about becoming the wealth that others needed.

CHAPTER XXVI

The Haunting of Unfinished Journeys

"The past is a shadow that follows us, not out of malice, but to remind us of who we were, so we may decide who we will become."

— Shree Shambav

The sky was a gentle canvas of soft oranges and pinks as the dawn broke over the horizon, the air thick with the weight of silence. The crew had gathered, and the ship anchored on the shore of Crystal Island. Aryan stood at the bow of the ship, eyes scanning the shimmering water, his mind far from the peaceful setting around him. They had come so far—so many islands, so many challenges faced, yet the emptiness within him had not lessened.

He should have felt fulfilled. After all, they had achieved what they had set out to do—the child was saved, the herb collected, the people grateful. But it wasn't enough. The treasure he had been searching for, the thing that had haunted his every step for years, remained elusive. And today, Joseph had asked him the question that lingered like a shadow, "Have you found your treasure chest?"

Aryan had shaken his head, the words caught in his throat, too heavy to speak. The treasure was not gold. It was never about wealth. It was a question of purpose. But for all his success, all the people he had helped, Aryan couldn't shake the feeling that he was lost in a world that had long moved on without him.

"Sir, have you found it?" Joseph asked again, his voice laced with an odd kind of curiosity.

"No," Aryan had said quietly, his eyes distant.

Peter, standing by Aryan, turned to Captain. "We've searched so much, tried so many avenues... the clues, the maps, the whispers of old traders and adventurers... It seems like the treasure is always just out of reach."

Captain's brows furrowed. "I've gone over all my diaries, my maps, the people I know. All my contacts... all those we've met who claimed to know something... It's all been dead ends."

The silence hung heavy, until Joseph spoke again, his voice soft yet filled with an undercurrent of something... deeper. "Perhaps the treasure you seek isn't a thing at all. Perhaps it is something you need to uncover inside yourself."

Joseph's words cut through the quiet like a sharp wind, but before Aryan could respond, Joseph continued, "Tomorrow, an old sailor will arrive here. He's spent his life roaming the oceans, traversing the most dangerous territories, and surviving in the harshest environments. He claims he's seen every kind of island, desert, every corner of the world. He may have some insight for you. Perhaps this is not the end of your journey, but a new beginning. A few more days may be worth it."

The idea of staying even longer troubled the Aryan. His soul longed to return home, to rest, to somehow find peace. But there was an unsettling feeling in his gut, a sense of unfinished business, and a pull toward something he couldn't define.

"Let's wait for the sailor, then," Captain had said with a quiet sigh, acknowledging Aryan's hesitance without pressing further. "There's something about this place... It doesn't feel finished. But if we leave now, will we always wonder what might have been?"

So they stayed. And they waited. But the sailor did not arrive the next day. Nor the next. Days passed, and still, there was no sign of the old man with the world-weary eyes and the stories of uncharted lands.

Joseph's concern began to grow. He had known this sailor for years, and never had he failed to arrive on time. He was a man who could predict storms, navigate through the wildest seas, and find his way through the darkest jungles. The absence of the sailor was not something Joseph took lightly.

"This is not like him," Joseph murmured to himself, walking back and forth outside his house. "He was supposed to be here days ago... Something isn't right."

The weight of waiting began to wear on everyone. Peter, though a man of few words, could sense the growing unease in Aryan. Despite the outward calm, the storms in Aryan's heart were far from quiet. He could feel the sharp edge of frustration rising, like the swell of an ocean before it broke against the shore.

Peter caught Aryan's gaze one evening as they sat together on the stone steps outside the house, looking out at the horizon. There was a tenderness in Peter's eyes that Aryan hadn't noticed before, an empathy that seemed to reach through the walls Aryan had built around himself.

"You've been kind to so many, Aryan," Peter said quietly, his voice low and filled with understanding. "You've given of yourself in ways most people couldn't even imagine. You've helped people across the seas, across islands. But… no one can help you find what you're looking for. Not even you."

Aryan's heart tightened, but he said nothing. Peter's words cut deeper than he expected. There was truth in them, sharp and unyielding. For so long, Aryan had believed that his purpose was to give—to give power, to give guidance, to give love. But in doing so, he had lost sight of his own needs. His own heart had been left in the shadows, and he wasn't sure how to bring it back to the light.

"Maybe…" Aryan started, his voice faltering, "Maybe the journey was never about finding that treasure. Maybe it's about finding myself along the way."

Peter didn't respond immediately, but his gaze softened. "Perhaps it's time you started looking for that treasure within, Aryan."

But as time went on, the sailor still did not arrive. Joseph's worry grew into something more palpable—something darker.

It wasn't just the absence of the man; it was the absence of the clarity they all sought. Was it fate? Or had the sailor truly met some tragic end?

Finally, the decision was made. They could not afford to wait any longer. With heavy hearts, Captain, Peter, Aryan, and the rest of the crew left the island, but there was no sense of triumph in their departure. It was as if they were leaving behind more than just the island.

CHAPTER XXVII

The Echo of the Unseen

"There are conversations held in the spaces between words, in the glances, in the pauses, in the things we choose not to say, and yet they speak volumes."

— Shree Shambav

The wind had begun to settle as the last traces of the day slipped away, leaving the world bathed in the soft, silvery light of the rising moon. Aryan stood outside, leaning against the rough-hewn stone of the small hut, his gaze lost in the vast expanse of the night sky above. The stars were endless, like a sea of light, distant and untouchable, each one a reminder of something far beyond his grasp. He had been staring at them for hours, his mind drifting through the same thoughts that had haunted him for years: the treasure, the purpose, the sense of being adrift.

Tonight, he felt an unfamiliar sense of peace, despite the storm that still raged within him. Perhaps it was the child they had saved, or the kindness of the people around him, or the hope that came with the successful journey. But beneath it all, there was something unresolved. That pull—the hunger for answers, the quest for meaning—had not faded.

As Aryan continued to watch the stars, the quiet of the night was suddenly disturbed by the sound of footsteps, heavy and hurried, coming from the direction of the woods. He straightened, his senses alert. There was something unfamiliar about the movement—urgent, almost desperate. In the distance, he saw figures silhouetted against the soft glow of the moon. They were running towards the hut, their outlines sharp against the dark backdrop of the island.

Before Aryan could call out, Davina appeared at the door, her face creased with concern. "Who are they?" she asked, her voice tight.

Aryan stepped forward, curiosity mingling with a sense of caution. He knew this island, its people, the rhythm of life here. Yet these men, with their heavy breathing and hurried steps, felt like an interruption—something foreign in the peace they had so long sought.

The men arrived at the doorstep, their faces shadowed but their intent clear. One of them, the leader, stepped forward, his breath ragged but his eyes burning with a mixture of desperation and resolve.

"We need to speak with Aryan," the man said, his voice rough as if it had been scraped raw by the journey.

Aryan stood motionless, puzzled. He could feel the weight of their presence pressing against the calm of the island night.

"Who are you?" Davina asked, her voice sharp, though there was a tremor beneath her words. She stepped closer to Aryan, her protective instinct toward him palpable. "What is this about?"

"We have been sent by Joseph," the man continued. "The sailor has arrived on our island. He has come to speak with Aryan. He wishes to meet with him."

The mention of Joseph's name struck a chord in Aryan's chest. Joseph, the man who had seen something in him, had always been a guiding light during these travels. The connection they shared had been a strange comfort, but now, with these men standing before him, there was an unsettled feeling creeping into his heart.

"Joseph?" Aryan repeated, trying to make sense of the urgency in their voices. "What does this mean?"

"He wants to speak with you, Aryan. He says it is urgent—something important. We were told to find you here."

Aryan's heart raced as memories flooded back. The sailor, who had been missing, the one who promised answers, the man who had seen the world and everything in it. What had he learned? What did he know? More than anything, Aryan knew that his own restless soul was caught in the undertow of this strange summons. It was as if the universe had decided that now, at this very moment, the path he had walked all these years—so full of questions, so fraught with uncertainty—was about to take a sharp turn into the unknown.

Davina, standing nearby, looked between Aryan and the men. "What should we do?" she asked, her voice a mixture of worry and caution. She had already seen too much of the uncertainty in Aryan's heart, too much of the restless pursuit that had driven him.

Aryan paused, staring at the men. Then, with a sigh, he made his decision. "We go," he said, his voice firm. There was no hesitation in his tone, no question of whether this was the right thing to do. His heart was already pulling him toward whatever lay beyond the horizon, to the answers that seemed just out of reach.

Peter and Captain, who had been watching from the shadows, approached. The Captain's brow furrowed in concern. "Are you sure about this, Aryan?" he asked, his voice low and filled with an unspoken question. "We've come so far. Should we not rest before heading back?"

But Peter, who had spent so many quiet hours observing Aryan, nodded gravely. "He's right. There's something calling him—something he needs to understand. We can't deny that."

Aryan turned toward them, his gaze steady but distant, the weight of years of searching pressing down on him. "I have to go. Whatever Joseph wants, whatever answers he holds, they are part of this journey. If I turn away now, I'll always wonder what I missed."

They all shared a moment of silence before the Captain finally spoke again, his voice soft but resolute. "Then we go together, as we always do."

The night felt unusually long as they prepared to leave. The gentle lapping of the waves against the shore, the rustling of the trees in the cool breeze—it was as if the island itself was holding its breath, waiting for what was to come.

As Aryan walked toward the boat that would carry them to Joseph's island, a strange calm washed over him. It was a calm that came not from certainty, but from the deep, unsettling sense that his life was on the edge of something—something he couldn't yet name.

The moonlight danced across the water as they made their way across the sea, the waves stirring under the hull, each ripple a whisper of what lay ahead. Aryan's heart thudded in his chest as he thought of Joseph, the sailor, and what they might learn in the coming hours.

The boat rocked gently, and Aryan turned to the horizon, watching as the island behind him slowly receded into the distance. He had no idea what was waiting for him, but for the first time in years, he felt a flicker of something he had long forgotten: hope.

CHAPTER XXVIII

The Path to Gorgons

"It is not the destination that shapes us, but the road we travel—each step, each stumble, each quiet triumph along the way."

— Shree Shambav

The next morning, the air was thick with anticipation as the small group of travellers prepared to venture toward the mysterious island that had haunted Aryan for so long. The sky was clear, but Aryan's heart felt heavy, a weight pulling him toward the unknown. The ocean stretched endlessly before them, vast and cold, mirroring the uncertainty in his soul. As the boat rocked gently, Aryan found himself lost in thought. His fingers brushed against the edges of the worn map, the paper frayed and aged with time, and he felt a flicker of hope and fear rising in his chest. He had come so far, but would this journey bring him the answers he desperately sought, or would it deepen the mystery, pulling him into a darker place of endless searching?

Silently, he prayed to the divine, hoping this time would be different. *Please, let this sailor be the key. Let him help me find what I've been seeking.*

As the boat drew closer to the island, Aryan's hands trembled slightly. His gaze fixed on the shoreline, where the silhouette of a solitary figure waited for them. Joseph stood with a welcoming smile, but there was an urgency in his eyes, a deep concern that Aryan could not ignore. He had placed his faith in Joseph's wisdom before, and now, standing at the threshold of this new phase of his journey, he hoped the man's belief in him would prove true once again.

The boat finally touched the shore with a gentle thud, and Aryan stepped off, his feet sinking into the soft sand. The air smelled of salt and earth, a strange mixture that both unsettled and grounded him. Joseph greeted him warmly, but his eyes betrayed a deeper worry. The time had come to confront the unknown, to face whatever awaited him in this place.

"Aryan," Joseph said, his voice calm but heavy with meaning, "I'm glad you've come. Let's see what we can do for you now. Perhaps this sailor has the answers."

As they made their way toward the gathering, Aryan's heart raced. The old sailor, Jack, sat on a rock nearby, his long white beard swaying gently in the breeze. His glasses were thick, his eyes magnified behind the lenses, yet there was a clarity in his gaze that struck Aryan immediately. The man's appearance—worn and weathered, as though he had lived through many storms—spoke of a life filled with untold stories. Jack's presence was like the silent force of the sea itself—enduring, strong, and full of wisdom.

Jack smiled when he saw Aryan and waved them over. "So, you've come," he said, his voice gruff but warm, as if he had been expecting this moment for a long time. He motioned for

Aryan to hand over the map, his wrinkled hands trembling slightly as he took it. "Let's see if this old map of yours holds any secrets."

Aryan handed the map over with a quiet nod, feeling a strange sense of finality in the action. The old sailor took out a magnifying glass and examined the paper with painstaking care. The map was tattered, edges curling from years of being folded and unfolded, yet the markings on it were still legible—a labyrinth of lines and symbols that only someone with experience could decode.

"What are you searching for, son?" Jack asked, eyes never leaving the map. His voice softened with a strange tenderness, as though speaking to a long-lost friend.

"I'm searching for a place," Aryan replied, his voice steady despite the storm of emotions inside him. "A place I've been chasing for years. A place I have dreamt of. A treasure… a legacy. I believe it holds the answers to everything I've been asking."

Jack nodded slowly, then leaned in closer, his gaze scanning the map again. "A treasure, eh? Let's see what this map tells us, then."

For a long while, the only sound was the faint rustling of the wind through the leaves and the rhythmic pounding of the waves against the shore. Then, with a grunt, Jack set the map down on the sand, his hands hovering over it as he began to sketch on the ground. The lines were fluid, instinctive, as if he had drawn this before, or as though the knowledge had been etched into his very being over the course of many lifetimes.

"This," Jack said, pointing to the rough sketch in the sand, "is what you're looking for." He began outlining the path—treacherous islands, vast stretches of dry land, a golden desert, and a solitary tree. His finger traced each landmark, the lines taking shape, becoming something real.

Aryan leaned in, and his breath caught in his chest. This was it. This was the place—the place from his dreams.

"This is the island you seek," Jack continued, his voice soft but resolute. "The island of Gorgons. It lies beyond Stardorph—an unforgiving land. You will cross the Gold Haven desert, where the winds can strip flesh from bone. And the tree," Jack said, his finger tracing the last symbol in the sand, "is the Twilight-Blossom. A tree that has stood for centuries, watching over all who dare to approach."

Aryan's heart raced. "But… is it possible? Is it real?" His voice trembled with the weight of years of searching. He had asked himself this question so many times, but now, with Jack's words confirming everything, it felt as though his entire life had led to this moment.

Jack chuckled softly, a raspy sound. "I've seen many men come and go, searching for this place. Most never return. The terrain is harsh, the elements unforgiving. When I was young, I travelled these lands with my grandfather. I remember one man—a man like you, determined, unyielding—he sought this treasure, but I don't believe he ever reached it. It's a dangerous place."

Joseph stepped forward, placing a hand on Aryan's shoulder. "We will go with you. We will ensure your safety. We will gather everything you need. The journey may be difficult, but you will not be alone."

Jack smiled again, his eyes twinkling with mischief. "One more adventure, I suppose," he said, shrugging. "We'll see if we make it. But mark my words, the road to Gorgons is not one for the faint of heart."

The next morning, preparations began in earnest. Food, water, supplies—everything was arranged for the gruelling journey ahead. Jack, Joseph, Aryan, and the rest of the group set off at dawn, their faces set with determination. They knew the path would not be easy, but for Aryan, this was no longer just about treasure. This was about finding something far deeper—a purpose, a truth, and a place that had called to him for so many years.

As they sailed toward the island of Gorgons, Aryan couldn't shake the feeling that he was stepping into something greater than himself. It was as if the island, with its harsh landscape and hidden secrets, was a reflection of his own journey—a journey that had taken him through darkness and light, through pain and hope. And now, at last, the time had come to face whatever awaited him in that forgotten place.

CHAPTER XXIX

Whispers of the Forgotten Land

"A man can fill his pockets with gold, yet if his soul remains empty, he is still a beggar in the grand marketplace of life."

— Shree Shambav

The voyage across the ocean was merciless. The ship groaned under the force of the winds, the sails billowing like wounded beasts, fighting against the rage of the sea. The waves crashed with fury, each one a reminder that nature, in all its power, cared nothing for the desires of men. But Jack, the old sailor, stood firm at the helm, his weathered hands gripping the wheel with the confidence of a man who had outlived a thousand storms. His keen eyes, dulled by age but sharpened by experience, read the winds like an old manuscript, guiding the vessel through the chaos.

After what felt like an eternity, the storm relented, leaving behind a sky streaked with orange and crimson as dawn touched the horizon. The air was heavy with salt and silence as they approached the island.

Gorgons.

A place whispered about in taverns and old sailor tales—a place few had seen and fewer had returned from.

As they set foot on the island, an unnatural stillness settled over them. The land before them was not welcoming—it was eerie, almost as if it resisted their presence. The trees twisted in unnatural shapes, their thick, thorny limbs reaching out like skeletal fingers. The air carried the scent of something rotten, a mixture of decay and damp earth. Birds with dark, soulless eyes circled above, their cries sharp and piercing, while insects the size of a man's fist crawled over rocks, their legs clicking against the ground in a sinister rhythm.

Captain Alistair surveyed the land, his sharp eyes scanning the bleak landscape. "I have travelled across a thousand shores," he muttered, his voice laced with unease, "but never have I stepped foot on a land that feels… cursed."

Aryan remained silent, his gaze locked on the horizon. His heart, though filled with determination, felt the weight of an invisible force pressing down on him. Was it fear? Or was it something else, something deeper—like the island itself was whispering to him in an ancient, forgotten tongue?

Despite the unease that gripped them all, they pressed on. Hours of trekking through the island's labyrinthine paths led them to a clearing—a meadow, untouched by the corruption surrounding it. A small stream weaved its way through the grass, the water glistening under the sun, a stark contrast to the gloom they had left behind. Relief washed over them as they fell to their knees, cupping the cool water in their hands, letting it soothe their parched throats and weary bodies.

That night, tents were erected, and guards were stationed, and though exhaustion pulled at their bones, sleep did not come easy. The night carried strange sounds—whispers in the wind, the rustling of unseen creatures, the distant echo of something unnatural moving in the darkness. But the day's toil had drained them, and eventually, one by one, they succumbed to sleep, the unease lingering like a phantom in their dreams.

The Next Day

As dawn's golden fingers stretched across the sky, they prepared for the journey ahead. The real challenge lay before them—the Stardorph wasteland, an unforgiving land where the earth was cracked and lifeless, a place that had swallowed many before them.

Jack, ever the strategist, studied the land with the keen eye of a man who had long made survival his craft. "There is a shorter route," he announced, his finger tracing a path on the map. "If we cut straight through, we can halve our time crossing the desert. But," he paused, looking at the group, "it's a gamble. The longer route offers shade and possible water sources. The shorter one... nothing but heat and dust."

Aryan stepped forward. "We take the shorter route. Every moment we lose brings us further from our goal."

No one questioned him.

With the sun climbing higher, they stepped into the wasteland. The first hour was bearable, the heat only an inconvenience. But as time passed, the land fought back. The air grew dry, their throats parched, and the cruel sun pressed against their backs like a merciless taskmaster.

The desert stretched endlessly before them, an ocean of sand and stone, its waves unmoving, its silence louder than any storm. Their boots sank into the soft earth, each step stealing more of their strength. Sweat dripped from their brows, soaking their clothes, but the air was so dry that it evaporated before it could bring relief.

They trudged on, their breath growing laboured, their legs heavy. Skeletons of past travellers lay scattered along their path—bleached bones half-buried in the sand, a grim reminder of the fate that awaited those who miscalculated the desert's cruelty.

Jack, sensing the growing weakness among the group, called for a halt.

"Tents up," he ordered. "We rest before the sun claims us."

They obeyed without argument. The makeshift camp provided little comfort, but the shade was salvation. They drank sparingly from their water supply, every drop a treasure. The meal was simple—dried meat and stale bread—but to them, it tasted like a king's feast.

As the sun dipped toward the horizon, painting the sky in hues of crimson and violet, they resumed their journey, pressing forward under the cooler embrace of dusk.

With the first sign of moonlight upon them, they reached the edge of Stardorph. Before them, stretching like an endless golden sea, lay the Gold Haven desert. And far beyond, hidden in the heart of the sands, the Twilight-Blossom tree awaited—

Aryan's final destination, the answer to years of longing, of searching, of haunting dreams.

As they settled for the night, Aryan gazed up at the starlit sky. The vastness of it all pressed upon him, reminding him how small he was in the grand scheme of things. He had travelled so far, endured so much, and yet, the greatest challenge still lay ahead.

The whispers of the desert called to him, carried by the wind.

Would the treasure he sought bring him peace?

Or would it be another mirage, slipping through his fingers like grains of sand?

CHAPTER XXX

The Phantom of the Dunes

"Chasing after a dream without knowing its meaning is like drinking salt water—each sip only deepens the thirst."

— Shree Shambav

The desert night was cold, a cruel contrast to the scorching heat of the day. The sands, once blistering, had turned into icy sheets beneath their feet. A hush had fallen over the camp, broken only by the distant howls of desert winds whispering secrets across the dunes.

The men, exhausted from their journey, lay wrapped in their cloaks, seeking warmth in the embrace of slumber. But Aryan remained awake. His thoughts, like restless spirits, refused to be silenced. He stared into the dark expanse of the sky, where stars shimmered like scattered diamonds—ancient and untouchable, much like the treasure he sought.

Then, from the silence, it came.

The faint, rhythmic pounding of hooves against the sand.

It started as a murmur in the distance, growing louder, more insistent—a storm of unseen riders approaching like shadows of death.

Aryan sat up instantly, his hand moving to his dagger. He turned toward Jack and Alistair, who had already stirred, their years of travel making them light sleepers.

The sound grew deafening.

Then, from the darkness, they emerged.

A dozen figures on horseback, their faces veiled beneath dark cloth, their eyes glinting beneath the moonlight like silent predators. The lead rider, wrapped in flowing black robes, reined his steed to a halt, his piercing gaze fixed on Aryan's group.

A sharp voice cut through the stillness.

"Drop your weapons."

The demand was met with tense silence. The air itself seemed to hold its breath.

Then, Aryan stepped forward, his voice calm but unwavering. "We carry no treasure." His gaze met the masked leader. "We seek one."

The man let out a deep, mocking laugh, his voice heavy with skepticism. "Treasure?" His men shifted uneasily as if the very word was forbidden. "You have crossed these lands in vain, traveller. My ancestors have ruled these dunes for four generations, and no gold, no relic, no treasure has ever been found."

Aryan's jaw tightened. "A dream took root in me, vivid and unshakable—a treasure hidden beyond the mountains, beyond the reach of ordinary men. Whether it is fate or mere illusion, I do not know."

The man's posture stiffened. He studied Aryan for a long moment before stepping down from his horse. His movements were slow, deliberate, as if weighed down by an unseen burden.

"Do you know my name?" the masked man asked.

Aryan shook his head.

The man removed his hood, revealing piercing eyes that seemed to burn with both wisdom and warning. His face was veiled in partial shadow, but the moonlight carved the lines of a man hardened by the desert, by the very land itself.

"They call me Nightshade," he said. "I exist only in the dark."

A shiver passed through the group. The name was not unfamiliar—stories had spread of a desert phantom, a figure who appeared only when the moon was high, a ruler of the forsaken lands.

Nightshade's men dismounted, forming a loose circle around Aryan's group, though no weapons were drawn. The standoff had shifted into something else—a silent, unspoken test of will.

Nightshade's gaze returned to Aryan. "Tell me," he said, "where does your dream lead you?"

Aryan did not hesitate. "Beyond Gold Haven desert. To the Twilight-Blossom tree."

A ripple passed through Nightshade's men—an unspoken reaction that spoke of fear, of stories untold.

Nightshade's face darkened. His voice, when he spoke, was not of mockery but of something graver. "The Twilight-Blossom tree?"

Aryan nodded.

Nightshade exhaled sharply. He turned his gaze toward the horizon as if seeing something beyond the darkness, something long buried in time.

"No one returns from there," he murmured. "No one."

Silence draped over them like a shroud. Even the wind seemed to falter.

"You ask me to turn back," Aryan said quietly. "But I have spent my life searching for something that haunts my every waking moment. How can I abandon it now?"

Nightshade's eyes locked onto Aryan's, searching, measuring.

Then, after a long pause, he spoke.

"If you wish to continue," he said, his voice heavy with foreboding, "then you will need more than courage. You will need to understand the cost of desire. The desert does not forgive, and neither does the past."

Aryan did not flinch. "Then let the desert test me."

CHAPTER XXXI

The Threshold of Destiny

"A single act of kindness ripples through time, touching lives in ways even the giver may never see."

— Shree Shambav

The morning air was crisp yet heavy with the scent of brewing tea as the sun cast golden hues over the endless dunes. The men of Nightshade, usually shadows of the desert, moved like ghosts, their movements swift and precise as they prepared tea over a small fire. Aryan sat quietly, the weight of years pressing upon him as he watched the steam rise from the clay cups. The warmth spread through his fingers, but it did little to calm the storm in his chest.

One of Nightshade's men stepped forward, his face partially hidden beneath a tattered hood. His voice wavered between disbelief and reverence. "You are Aryan, aren't you?"

Nightshade turned abruptly, his keen eyes narrowing. "Karl, how do you know him?"

Karl took a step closer, his expression softened by the weight of memory. "Because he saved my life," he said, his voice carrying the burden of gratitude. "Many years ago, I was sentenced for stealing bread to feed my starving son, Sam. The law was merciless, but he—" Karl pointed at Aryan with trembling hands, "—he stood before them, and pleaded for my freedom. He said, 'A man who steals for greed is a thief, but a man who steals for his child is a father.' Because of him, I am here today."

A hush fell upon the group. The men of Nightshade, hardened by the desert, exchanged glances. It was rare to find kindness in men who chased treasure and ghosts.

Nightshade exhaled slowly. "A man of such integrity does not search for treasure to fill his pockets," he said, his voice thoughtful. "You chase something else… something deeper." He turned to his men. "Aryan is one of us now. We will help him."

With their guidance, Aryan and his companions pressed forward, their journey pushing them past the cruelest stretch of the Gold Haven desert. The land burned beneath their feet, the air thick with heat, the wind whispering warnings only the desert-born could understand. Yet, Nightshade and his men knew the path, their instincts honed by years of navigating the shifting sands.

And then, as the sun lowered behind them, Nightshade stopped his horse and pointed ahead. "There," he said.

Aryan followed the direction of his gaze.

A lone tree stood defiant against the endless dunes—its gnarled branches reaching towards the sky like the hands of a forgotten deity. The *Twilight-Blossom Tree*—the symbol that had haunted his dreams, the landmark his soul had chased through time.

Aryan's heart pounded, each beat echoing the years of longing, the endless nights spent tracing old maps, the faces of those who had doubted him, those who had walked beside him, and those he had lost. The journey was nearing its end.

Nightshade's voice was solemn. "This is where we leave you. The place ahead… it is not kind to those who enter. We will wait here for your return." His gaze met Aryan's. "If you return."

Aryan swallowed, the weight of fate pressing against him. He turned to Captain Alistair, Peter, and Joseph, each of them standing firm beside him.

"We ride," Aryan said.

And with that, they pushed forward, the last stretch of the journey standing between them and destiny.

CHAPTER XXXII

The Mirror of Truth

"The greatest treasure is not buried beneath the earth, but reflected in the eyes of a man who has truly understood himself."

— *Shree Shambav*

The wind howled through the desolate expanse, carrying whispers of forgotten souls. As Aryan sat beneath the gnarled branches of the **Twilight-Blossom Tree**, exhaustion clung to him like a heavy cloak. His journey had been long, spanning years of hardship, battles fought in the name of an elusive dream. And now, here he was—within reach of the treasure that had haunted him since childhood.

Captain Alistair, Peter, and Joseph—his steadfast companions—had collapsed the moment they stepped into the tree's shadow. Their bodies lay motionless on the cracked, golden earth, their breath shallow. Panic rose in Aryan's chest like a tide, but before he could move, an eerie silence settled upon the land. The very air thickened, wrapping around him like an unseen presence.

A deep voice, ancient and commanding, echoed from nowhere and everywhere at once.

"Finally, you are here, my child."

Aryan's heart pounded against his ribs. He turned swiftly, his hands trembling, but no figure stood before him.

"Who are you?" he demanded. His voice cracked under the weight of uncertainty.

"The one who has always been waiting."

The words sent a shiver down Aryan's spine. His pulse quickened as the voice continued.

"Your treasure is behind this tree. But listen well—never reveal its truth to anyone. Some treasures are meant only for the ones who dare to seek them."

The wind howled once more, the voice fading like mist in the morning sun. For a long moment, Aryan remained frozen, his breath uneven. When he finally gathered the courage, he stepped behind the tree.

Beneath its twisted roots, hidden under layers of hardened earth, lay an old, rusted chest. His fingers, now weathered with age, clawed at the dirt, digging with a desperate urgency. Every scrape of his nails against the soil felt like a lifetime slipping through his grasp.

At last, the chest was free. He hesitated.

This was the moment he had lived for. The moment that had shaped his every decision, stolen his sleep, and whispered promises of purpose into his ear.

With bated breath, he unlatched the ancient lock and pushed open the lid.

Inside, there were no gold coins, no shimmering jewels, and no divine relics. Only **a mirror and a single parchment.**

Confusion clutched at Aryan's chest. His hands shook as he lifted the mirror, its silver surface worn with time. His own reflection stared back at him—his once-youthful face now lined with the etchings of countless years, his eyes sunken with longing, his hair a fading silver.

He had grown old searching for this moment.

His throat tightened. The dreams of a child, the ambition of a young man, the perseverance of an adult—all had led him here. And now, at the edge of revelation, time had stolen from him what he could never reclaim.

His gaze fell upon the parchment. He unfolded it with trembling fingers, his breath hitching as he read the words inscribed upon it:

"You have always carried the true treasure within you."

Tears welled in Aryan's eyes. His vision blurred as the weight of realisation pressed down upon him like a mountain. **It was never about gold. Never about riches.**

The true treasure was the journey itself.

The people he had met. The lives he had touched. The lessons learned through hardship. The friendships that had carried him through storms and deserts. The love he had given and received, though fleeting.

A broken laugh escaped his lips, bitter and sorrowful. He had spent his entire life chasing a dream, never realising that the greatest riches had been with him all along.

How cruel. And yet, how beautiful?

He placed the parchment back in the chest with reverence, as though returning a sacred truth to its slumber. The mirror, he held for a moment longer, watching himself as if for the first time. Then, gently, he closed the lid.

The hunt was over.

Wiping his tear-streaked face, Aryan turned back to his fallen companions. With his hands still trembling, he found the small bottle of water the voice had spoken of. He uncorked it and sprinkled its cool drops upon Captain Alistair, Peter, and Joseph.

One by one, they stirred, gasping as if waking from a long slumber.

Peter clutched his head. **"What... what happened?"**

Aryan forced a smile. **"You were merely asleep. We can go home now."**

Joseph looked around, bewildered. **"And the treasure? Did you find it?"**

Aryan hesitated. Then, he exhaled a deep breath and nodded. **"Yes... I found it."**

Captain Alistair frowned. **"And? What was it?"**

Aryan looked towards the horizon, where the first golden rays of dawn painted the endless sky. The world was vast, more than he had ever known.

He smiled, a quiet, knowing smile.

"It was everything I was searching for."

And with that, Aryan left the treasure buried beneath the tree.

For he finally understood...

The greatest treasures are not those we seek—but those we live.

CHAPTER XXXIII

The Final Journey Home

"A traveler may cross a thousand lands, but if he does not journey within, he remains forever lost."

— Shree Shambav

The waves of the **Gold Haven Desert** rolled behind them like an unforgiving sea of golden dust, whispering echoes of their perilous journey. The **Twilight-Blossom Tree** faded into the horizon, becoming nothing more than a distant silhouette against the setting sun. But the questions remained, lingering like ghosts in the minds of those who had accompanied Aryan through the brutal passage of fate.

Captain Alistair, ever the realist, narrowed his eyes at Aryan as they rode back. His boots crunched against the desert sand, his hands gripping the reins of his horse tightly. The answer Aryan had given unsettled him. **"It is within me,"** Aryan had said. But how could a man risk everything, traverse storms, battle uncertainty, and defy death itself—only to claim the treasure was something intangible?

Alistair pulled his horse closer to Aryan's side. The moon was now rising, casting silver light upon the weary travelers.

"Aryan," the Captain spoke, his voice rough but sincere. "Enough of riddles. I've followed you through lands where the sun itself is a tyrant, where the wind howls like lost spirits. I watched men fall and rise for this journey. Now tell me, truly, have you found your treasure?"

Aryan turned to him, his eyes reflecting something deeper than mere contentment—something eternal, as if the universe itself had whispered its secrets to him.

"Yes," Aryan said simply, a small, knowing smile playing on his lips.

Peter, who had been silent for most of the journey back, frowned. **"Then where is it?"**

Aryan slowed his horse, exhaling deeply as he gazed upon the horizon, the last vestiges of twilight fading into the dark abyss of the night.

"It is within me."

Silence.

Peter let out a frustrated sigh. "Aryan, I respect you, but please—what does that even mean?"

Joseph, who had been listening quietly, merely observed Aryan's face. He had known this man for years—his pain, his ambition, his longing. And now, as he looked at him, he saw something different. Not just satisfaction—but peace.

Joseph smiled to himself. **He has found something far greater than gold.**

Peter, though still puzzled, was beginning to understand.

They continued their journey back until they reached the outskirts of the desert, where **Nightshade** and his men were waiting, their figures like dark phantoms against the dunes. The leader of the desert outlaws stepped forward, his piercing eyes watching Aryan with curiosity.

"Well?" Nightshade asked, arms crossed over his chest. **"Did you find it?"**

Aryan nodded.

"And where is it?" Nightshade pressed.

Aryan smiled, the same mysterious, unwavering smile. **"It is within me."**

Nightshade scoffed. "Within you?" He shook his head, stepping closer, his voice dropping. "You are an influential man, Aryan. A man of power, intelligence. You would not have risked life and limb for something you already possessed. Why take such a treacherous, life-threatening journey for something that was always within you?"

Aryan's gaze softened. The night wind rustled through their cloaks, dust swirling around their boots.

"Because only through the journey," Aryan said, "do we realise what was within us all along."

Nightshade frowned, deep in thought. Around them, his men murmured, their curiosity piqued. But Nightshade remained silent. Something in Aryan's words unsettled him—not because he did not understand, but because deep down, he did.

Nightshade finally sighed, shaking his head with a small chuckle. "I don't know if you're a wise man or a madman, Aryan."

Aryan chuckled in return. "Perhaps both."

A pause. Then Aryan turned to Nightshade, his expression growing serious. "You have done much for me, Nightshade. You and your men. I owe you my life."

Nightshade waved a dismissive hand. "We only did what was right."

Aryan's eyes softened. "That is what makes it so valuable."

There was a brief silence before Aryan continued. "Come with me, Nightshade. There is a place for you where I come from."

At this, Nightshade stilled. His men looked at him in surprise. The once-feared bandit of the desert offered a different life? A life beyond these forsaken sands?

Nightshade hesitated. "You don't know what you're offering, Aryan. My hands have done things I cannot undo."

Aryan met his gaze, unwavering. "A man is not the sum of his worst deeds, Nightshade. You may have lost your way once, but I see in you the same boy that Joseph once played with. A boy who could still choose a different path."

Joseph, hearing this, turned to Nightshade in shock. "You... you knew me?"

Nightshade lowered his gaze. "I did. Long ago. When we were children. I turned to shadows, while you walked in the light."

Joseph swallowed hard. "You should have told me."

Nightshade smirked faintly. "I was ashamed."

Aryan placed a firm hand on Nightshade's shoulder. **"Shame is a prison. Redemption is a door. You decide which one you walk through."**

Nightshade looked away, staring at the horizon, lost in thought. He had never imagined a life beyond the desert. Beyond survival.

Finally, he sighed. **"Let me think on it."**

Aryan nodded, understanding.

By morning, they reached the shore where their boat awaited. The sea stretched infinitely before them, calm and endless. The home they had left behind now called them back, but none of them were the same men who had first set sail.

Aryan turned one last time to Nightshade and his men. **"Thank you, my friends."**

Nightshade nodded, his expression unreadable. As Aryan and his companions boarded their boat, the desert wind carried one last whisper:

"You already repaid us, Aryan... by reminding us who we once were."

As the sails caught the wind, pushing them toward home, Aryan stood at the bow of the ship, watching the horizon. The journey was ending.

But another was about to begin.

CHAPTER XXXIV

The Journey Ends, The Journey Begins

"In the end, all roads lead not to a place, but to a person—the one we were always meant to become."

— Shree Shambav

The sea whispered its final farewell as Aryan and his companions stepped onto familiar shores. The journey that had stolen years of his life, tested the limits of his soul, and carved truths into his being was now behind him. But the weight of it, the meaning of it, would never leave.

For a day, they rested on the island before their final stretch home. As Aryan stood by the cliffs, watching the sun set into the infinite horizon, Joseph approached him.

Joseph had always respected Aryan, but now, that respect had transformed into something deeper—a silent reverence for a man who had defied fate, who had given meaning to suffering, who had pursued a dream even at the cost of his own life.

He stood beside Aryan, the ocean wind brushing against them. **"Your dream is fulfilled,"** Joseph said, his voice quiet but firm. **"But dreams like yours… they change a man."**

Aryan smiled; his gaze lost in the waves. **"Maybe the journey was the dream, Joseph. Maybe I never truly chased a treasure, but something greater—the understanding that it was never outside of me."**

Joseph studied him for a moment before nodding. His respect for Aryan had grown **tenfold. A man who walks toward his dream despite knowing he may never reach it—that is a rare man.**

The next morning, Aryan and his team made their way to Crystal Island, where Davina and her father greeted them warmly. The once-dying child now ran barefoot along the shore, laughter bubbling from his small chest.

Davina clasped Aryan's hands, her eyes filled with gratitude. **"You are not just a man, Aryan,"** she whispered. **"You are a miracle to those who need one."**

Aryan only smiled. **"I am simply a man who tries to be what I wish the world was."**

As they left the island, they travelled for two long days before finally arriving home. The familiar land stretched before him—the towering gates of his estate, the golden domes glistening under the morning sun. The place where his journey had begun so many years ago.

The Sultan's men, who had faithfully accompanied him, bowed low. Aryan turned to them, his heart full of gratitude. "You have been my shield, my strength. You carried me through storms, deserts, and unknown lands."

He took a small pouch of silver coins and handed it to them. "Take this not as payment, but as a token of my gratitude. You did not serve me—you stood with me. And for that, I will always be grateful."

The men, hardened by war and duty, bowed deeply. "It was an honor, my Lord."

That night, as Aryan sat in his grand palace, Captain Alistair and Peter stood before him, ready to take their leave.

The Captain, a man who had seen countless battles and braved the mightiest storms, looked at Aryan and, for the first time, his voice trembled with emotion. "I have travelled the world, Aryan. I have met kings and warlords, thieves and scholars. But never have I met a man like you."

"Despite your power, your wealth, your fame—you remain humble. You have given more than you have ever taken. You planted kindness and compassion wherever you stepped, and now the world returns that kindness to you. This journey with you will remain the most cherished in my life."

Peter, the loyal friend who had walked beside Aryan through danger and doubt, placed a firm hand on his shoulder. His voice was thick with emotion.

"I have always been proud to call you my friend, Aryan. But now... I am honoured."

The two men turned and left, their figures disappearing into the moonlit streets.

That night, Aryan lay in the lavish comfort of his palace, yet his heart felt lighter than it ever had.

Years of searching, of running, of hoping, had come to an end.

Now, it was time for the final journey.

A journey not across deserts or seas, but back to where it all began.

Back to his home.

Back to the faces he had longed to see—his parents, his love, his friends, the elders who had once guided him, the place where his childhood laughter still echoed in the wind.

As sleep took him, a single tear escaped his eye.

Not of sadness.

But of fulfilment.

The treasure hunt was over. Finally, Aryan was going home.

CHAPTER XXXV
The Return Home

"He conquered lands, built empires, and amassed riches, yet the only thing he could not buy back was time."

— Shree Shambav

The morning sun painted golden hues across the vast sky as Aryan stood on the balcony of his palatial home. The wind carried whispers of the past, and with each breath, he felt the weight of his journey settle within him. It was time to return home—not to the walls that surrounded him, but to the place where his soul had first learned to dream.

He summoned Kenji, the most trusted and revered figure in his business. Kenji was a man of quiet wisdom, his silver hair marking years of experience, his eyes sharp as if reading the unspoken thoughts of men.

"Kenji, I entrust everything to you while I am away," Aryan said, his voice steady.

Kenji nodded, folding his hands before him. "You have built this empire with integrity. It will stand firm until you return."

With everything arranged, Aryan set forth on his journey. The road stretched endlessly ahead, but for the first time, it was not a path toward conquest—it was a path home.

Seeing Beauty with Closed Eyes

As Aryan travelled, he began to reflect on what beauty truly meant.

The world had often told him that beauty was in gold and silk, in power and wealth. But as he closed his eyes, the images that surfaced were not those of jewels or palaces. Instead, he saw Mira's eyes—deep, filled with love, the only place where his soul ever felt truly seen. He saw his mother's hands, roughened from work but gentle in their touch. His father's shoulders, hunched under the weight of responsibility, yet never breaking. He saw Rohan's laughter in the wind, Suraj's wisdom in the stillness of a night sky, and Baba Govind's words, which had shaped him more than any treasure ever could.

Beauty had never been in what he possessed. It had always been the people who had touched his life.

The Essence of Beauty

One evening, they camped by a river. As the moon cast silver reflections on the water, one of the younger guards, Elias, turned to Aryan.

"Master Aryan, you have seen so much of the world. Tell me, is beauty something we see, or something we feel?"

Aryan smiled, looking at the boy who reminded him of his youthful wonder. "Tell me, Elias, when you look at this river, do you find it beautiful?"

Elias nodded. "Yes, it shimmers like glass under the moonlight."

Aryan picked up a stone and threw it into the water. Ripples distorted the reflection. "And now?"

Elias hesitated. "It is still beautiful, but... different."

"Exactly," Aryan said. "Beauty is not in the river itself. It is in the way we choose to see it. Sometimes, we must close our eyes to see what is truly beautiful. Not in perfection, but in the way something makes us feel."

The Chase for Perfection

The journey continued through villages and towns, each place a reminder of how much he had once longed for wealth and prestige. He had spent years chasing perfection—flawless victories, unbreakable legacies. But was it all an illusion?

In one village, an old woman sat outside her modest home, her wrinkled hands weaving a garland of wildflowers. She looked up and smiled at Aryan.

"You have the eyes of a man who has searched for something his whole life," she said.

Aryan paused, intrigued. "And do you think I have found it?"

The woman chuckled. "That depends. Did you seek something real, or just the illusion of perfection?"

Aryan thought of his journey—the battles fought, the sleepless nights, the endless hunger to achieve more. And yet, what had filled his heart with peace was not gold, but the friendships he had formed, the love he had given and received.

"Perhaps I was searching for something I had all along," he admitted.

The woman handed him the garland. "Then you are a wise man, for most never realise that."

Recognising Beauty in Ourselves

As they neared his homeland, Aryan saw his reflection in a still pond. He had changed. His face bore lines of wisdom, his hair carried streaks of silver. For so long, he had judged himself by what he had achieved, by the admiration of others. But was that true beauty?

Joseph, who had travelled with him, placed a hand on Aryan's shoulder. "Do you know what makes you different, Aryan? You see the beauty in others. But have you ever looked at yourself with the same eyes?"

Aryan looked away. "I have never thought about it."

Joseph smiled. "Then it is time you did. A man who has given so much to the world must also see the beauty in himself."

Redefining Beauty

The final stretch of the journey was through the golden fields of his childhood. The village was visible in the distance, his home just beyond the hills.

Nightshade's words echoed in his mind. "Why risk so much if the treasure was always within you?"

Aryan finally understood. Beauty was not in the destination but in the journey. Not in riches, but in the people who stood beside him. Not in a flawless life, but in the imperfections that made it meaningful.

CHAPTER XXXVI

The Last Promise

"Love does not count years, nor measure distances—it simply waits, unwavering, even when the body can no longer endure the weight of time."

— Shree Shambav

As they approached the village, Aryan felt an unease creeping into his heart. The place he had once called home was just beyond the hill, but something within him whispered that time had not been kind to it. His heartbeat quickened, his breath grew uneven, and every step forward felt like he was stepping into a past that no longer belonged to him.

Finally, the village came into view. Aryan froze in his tracks.

The once-thriving land of his childhood was now a shadow of itself. The fields that once swayed with golden grains lay barren, cracked by years of neglect. The river that had once been the lifeblood of the village was nothing more than a thin stream struggling to find its way. The houses, those that still stood, bore the scars of time—crumbling walls, broken doors, and silence where once there had been laughter.

Joseph, who had travelled alongside Aryan through storms and deserts, placed a hand on his shoulder. "Are you alright?"

Aryan could not answer. He was already walking ahead, searching for faces he knew, for voices he remembered.

His first destination was Rohan's house. Rohan—his childhood friend, the one who had stood by him in his youth, who had dreamed with him beneath the open skies. But as he reached the house, his steps faltered. The home was no longer a home; it was a ruin, its wooden beams collapsed inwards, its courtyard overtaken by weeds. No sounds of children playing, no scent of fresh bread from the kitchen.

A frail figure moved slowly across the road, hunched over a wooden staff. His face was weathered by age, his beard white like winter's frost. Aryan hesitated, then called out, "Elder, may I ask—what happened to the people who lived here? I am looking for my friend, Rohan."

The old man turned, his tired eyes scanning Aryan's face. He squinted, as if trying to place him. "Rohan? That name I have not heard in years."

Aryan stepped closer, desperation in his voice. "Where is he?"

The elder chuckled, though it was devoid of joy. "You look like a man of great wealth. Rohan was poor. How could you be his friend?"

Aryan did not care for the old man's assumptions. "Where is he?" he repeated, his voice firmer now.

The old man sighed, his grip tightening on his staff. "Rohan died a decade ago… taken by a disease. There was no one to save him."

The words felt like a dagger piercing through Aryan's heart. His legs wavered beneath him, and he took a deep breath before asking, "What about Suraj?"

The old man's brows knitted together. "Suraj? He passed away two years ago. Age and sorrow took him."

Aryan's heart pounded. His chest felt heavy, as if the weight of years lost was pressing down on him. His lips trembled as he forced himself to ask, "Baba Govind?"

The old man did not hesitate this time. "He left this world even earlier than the others. He was wise, but even wisdom cannot keep death away."

A deep silence stretched between them. The world around Aryan blurred, and for the first time in years, he felt truly lost. His journey had been long, filled with dangers, victories, and revelations—but this, this was a loss he had not prepared for.

Joseph stepped forward, gently touching Aryan's shoulder. "Aryan, please, let's sit for a while. You need to breathe."

Aryan did not argue. He walked to a shaded area near an old tree and sank to the ground. He closed his eyes, the faces of his loved ones flashing before him—Rohan's laughter, Suraj's wise counsel, Baba Govind's gentle voice. And then another face appeared before him, one that made his heart clench—Mira.

Was she still alive? Did she still remember him? Did she wait, or had she moved on, believing him to be nothing more than a ghost of the past?

He clenched his fists, his lips moving in a silent prayer. "Divine, I have lost so much. Please, let my parents be alive. Let Mira be safe. Let those who remain be well. I ask for nothing else."

The wind carried his whisper across the village, as if the heavens themselves were listening.

The final treasure he had searched for was never gold, never riches—it was love, it was home, it was the people who made life worth living. And now, he feared that what he had truly sought was already lost.

But still, he had to move forward. The road ahead was not yet over.

CHAPTER XXXVII

The Journey's True End

"Some promises are not meant to be fulfilled in this life, but in the quiet spaces between hearts, where love never fades."

— Shree Shambav

A sudden stillness settled over Aryan, as if time itself had frozen. His fingers curled into the dry earth beneath him, his body trembling, not from the long journey, but from the weight of the words Ramji had just spoken.

His parents… gone.

A slow, hollow ache spread through his chest. All these years, he had dreamt of returning, of seeing their wrinkled smiles, of falling at their feet, of hearing his mother's voice call him her "little warrior" just one more time. The thought of them waiting for him, growing older, wondering if their son would ever return—it was unbearable. He had carried the dream of reunion like a flame in the darkness, and now, with one breath, it had been extinguished forever.

Joseph placed a steadying hand on Aryan's shoulder. "Aryan…" he began, but Aryan held up a hand.

"Let me... breathe this moment," he whispered, his voice raw.

Ramji, too, sat in silence, his old, weary eyes reflecting the sorrow of time. "They spoke of you often, Aryan. Your mother, until her last breath, believed you would return. Your father... he was a proud man, but he softened in his final days. He told me... he wished he had held you back, but also, that he was proud that his son had the courage to chase what he believed in."

Aryan closed his eyes, his chest rising and falling with heavy breaths. "I chased a dream... but I never realised what I left behind," he murmured.

Then, after what felt like an eternity, he lifted his head, his vision blurry with unshed tears. "You said... Mira is alive?" His voice was barely above a whisper, as if afraid the truth might slip through his fingers.

Ramji nodded. "She never married. She waited, Aryan. Through years of famine, through the pain of losing her family, through the silence of your absence. Many asked for her hand, but she refused. She still waits in that small house at the edge of the village... though she is not the same girl you left behind. Time has not been kind."

Aryan inhaled sharply, his hands pressing against his face. "And I let her wait," he murmured. "I let her wait all these years... for a man who didn't even know himself."

Joseph spoke, his voice firm yet kind. "She made her choice, Aryan. You must now make yours. Go to her. Or leave, forever haunted by what might have been."

Aryan rose slowly, his heart hammering against his ribs. His legs felt weak as if the weight of his journey had only now begun to press upon him.

"I need to see her," he whispered.

"Where is she?"

Ramji's eyes, old and wise, softened with sorrow. "Come with me," he said simply.

Elias and the others, who had silently witnessed the unfolding storm of emotions, wiped their misty eyes. Even hardened men—men who had sailed rough seas, crossed merciless deserts, and seen death in its cruelest form—felt something stir deep in their souls.

Together, they walked. The village was eerily silent, as if time itself had slowed. The dust rose in soft spirals with each step, and the once-familiar paths now seemed foreign to Aryan. Every corner held a memory—a childhood race, a whispered secret, a stolen moment of laughter under the banyan tree. But now, the banyan tree was gone. Just like so much else.

Then, they stopped.

A small hut stood before them, alone, with no trees to shade it. The walls were cracked, the thatched roof weathered by years of sun and storm. It was as if the very breath of life had left this place.

Ramji walked to the door and tapped it gently.

The wooden creak echoed in the still air. Inside, there was movement—slow, deliberate.

And then, she appeared.

Mira.

Her frail form leaned against the doorframe, her body unsteady, her once luminous eyes now sunken, holding the weight of years gone by. She was wrapped in a simple, faded shawl, her hands trembling as she lowered herself onto the veranda's wooden step.

Aryan's breath caught in his throat.

This was not the Mira he had left behind. This was a woman whom time had tested, a soul that had endured far more than he could fathom.

He took a step forward, then another, until he was close enough to kneel at her feet.

"Mira," he whispered.

She blinked at him, tilting her head slightly, her tired eyes searching his face. She did not speak.

Aryan's lips trembled. "I have returned," he said, his voice breaking.

Still, she stared, silent.

A tear rolled down Aryan's cheek. His hands found hers—thin, delicate, cold. He pressed them to his forehead. "I am Aryan," he choked. "I have come to take you, as I promised. I never left you behind. I always carried you in my heart."

Mira's lips parted into the faintest of smiles, a smile filled with something deeper than sorrow—acceptance.

"You never truly left," she murmured, her voice barely above a whisper.

Aryan swallowed hard. "Mira, come with me. Let me take care of you. Let me—"

She raised a trembling hand and cupped his cheek, silencing him.

"I am happy," she said softly. "That you have finally found your treasure."

Her words struck him like lightning.

He had spent a lifetime chasing a dream, running towards something that always felt just out of reach. And now, here, in the presence of the one person who had always been his greatest truth, he realised the treasure had never been buried in gold or hidden beyond distant mountains.

It had always been here.

Mira exhaled shakily, her breath faltering.

"Water," she whispered.

Aryan scrambled, reaching for the small flask at his waist. He carefully lifted it to her lips, watching as she sipped with effort.

A sigh escaped her, almost peaceful. She leaned forward, her fragile body pressing against his chest.

"I waited for this moment," she whispered against him. "I knew… you would come."

And then, a silence deeper than any Aryan had ever known.

Her head rested against his shoulder. The weight of her body grew still. The rise and fall of her breath… ceased.

The world around him blurred. The sky, the ground, the voices of his companions—it all faded into nothingness. He held her close, his arms tightening around her, as if he could will her soul back into her body. But there was no stopping time.

A soft breeze passed through the village, lifting the dust, rustling the tattered fabric hanging from doorways. The wind carried her spirit into the great unknown.

Joseph stepped forward, placing a gentle hand on Aryan's shoulder, but no words were spoken. No words were enough.

And at that moment, Aryan understood.

The greatest treasure was never gold nor power. It was love. It was understanding. It was the moments we share, the people who shaped us, the pain that taught us, and the journeys that showed us what was always within.

Was the journey ever about the treasure, or was the treasure the journey itself?

After seeking for so long, how do we know when we have truly arrived?

Aryan held Mira for a long time, until the stars blinked awake in the night sky. Until the weight of all the years settled into his soul. Until he was ready to face the truth.

He had returned home.

But home… had already left him.

Life Coach and Philanthropist

Shree Shambav is the visionary founder of the Shree Shambav Ayur Rakshita Foundation (www.shambav-ayurrakshita.org). He founded this institution with a lofty goal: to recognise human identity across gender, ethnicity, and nationality. Through this organisation, he wants to assist all communities in realising their full potential and the intrinsic beauty of life.

Shree Shambav, a Life Coach, is dedicated to supporting people on their journeys of self-discovery and empowerment. He assists people in discovering who they are, determining what inspires and drives them, and overcoming limiting ideas. His approach clarifies what one wants in life, assisting people through goal-setting and a step-by-step process for achieving them. He empowers people to make deliberate and responsible decisions, allowing them to identify their blind spots and evolve as individuals via the use of numerous strategies and tools.

The foundation's bold, uncompromising, and compassionate ventures are always aimed at initiating the "Inner Transformation" process. They focus on spiritual growth, personal growth, and self-healing while emphasising that true progress lies in "Inclusive Growth and Co-existence." This philosophy drives all their initiatives, encouraging a holistic approach to development and well-being.

Under Shree Shambav's leadership, the foundation has launched several impactful movements:

Shree Shambav Green Movement: This mission is to create a healthy, green, and clean earth through responsible water conservation and greening initiatives. The movement strives to make the world a green paradise by encouraging sustainable living and environmental responsibility.

Shree Shambav Vidya Vedhika (Vizhuthugal): This project aims to help students and children by offering training, books, stationery, and uniforms. It aims to provide the next generation with the tools and resources they need to excel both academically and personally.

Shree Shambav and his foundation exemplify the spirit of compassion, transformation, and inclusive growth via their work, which has a profound impact on individuals and communities around the world. His work exemplifies the power of acknowledging and nourishing the human spirit, creating a world in which everyone can reach their full potential and appreciate the beauty of life.

ACKNOWLEDGEMENTS

To my grandfathers, grandmothers, mothers, fathers, aunts, uncles, neighbours, sisters, brothers, friends, and teachers they poured in endless moral stories, retellings of Ramayana, Mahabharata, Puranas, Upanishads, and so on.

My teachers, neighbours, and kindred souls. Who provided us with a stage to perform wonderful Puranic stories and were gracious enough to acknowledge our efforts.

The artists and translators of epics have served as a source of inspiration, invigorating our spirits, making these works accessible, and enabling us to grasp the profound depths and deeper dimensions they contain.

I also cherish the stimulating conversations; I had with my wonderful mothers, Punitha Muniswamy and Uma Devi.

Our family's youngest member, Aadhya, who always overwhelmed me with questions, inspired this book.

I would likewise prefer to express gratitude to Mr Sivakumar, Mrs Roopa Sivakumar, Mr Akshaya Rajesh, Ms Akshatha Rajesh, Ms Apeksha Prabhu, Mr Akanksh Prabhu, Mr Nikash Sarasambi, and Mrs Spoorthi Nikash for their valuable inputs.

I must thank Mr Rajesh, Mr Savan Prabhu, Mrs Revathi Rajesh, Mrs Rajani Sarasambi, and Mrs Manju Reshma, who encouraged me and often suggested writing a book. Their unwavering belief that I had something valuable to offer kept me going during my writing sessions.

Love you all,

Shree Shambav

www.shambav.org

shreeshambav@gmail.com

www.ingramcontent.com/pod-product-compliance
Lightning Source LLC
LaVergne TN
LVHW091539070526
838199LV00002B/131